"Comprehensive research and strategic planning are indispensable for future real estate success. The Swanepoel Trends Report represents the gold standard for third party independent scholarship pertaining to this all-important process."

Gino Blefari, *CEO, HSF Affiliates*

"The Swanepoel Trends Report is one of the most important and influential analyses available in real estate. I always enjoy reading it, and it helps shape the future of our industry. Thanks to Stefan and the entire team at T3 Sixty for the hard work that goes into this report. Our industry is grateful for it."

Spencer Rascoff, CEO, Zillow Group

"It's the best consolidated market intel available and great tool to use to ponder change, innovation and the industry."

Matthew Consalvo, CEO, Arizona Regional MLS

"The Swanepoel Trends Report refines the way I view the industry. It's required reading for my entire board of directors."

Art Carter, CEO, CRMLS

"I have read it every year since it's come out. As an association CEO, the identification of trends in the annual Report helps us deliver timely and relevant services and information that better meets the needs and expectations of the brokerage community."

Travis Kessler, CEO, Texas Association of Realtors

"We greatly value the Swanepoel Trends Report. I have always felt Stefan's work is critically important to our industry because of his unique insights and desire to go beyond the metrics we all routinely look at. While there is quite a lot of industry discussion about disruptors, impact of technology and the emergence of millennials, it challenges us to think differently and offers unique ideas, suggestions and potential solutions."

Charlie Young, President & CEO, Coldwell Banker Real Estate

"It's what you read if you want to be in the know in real estate."

Terrie Suit, CEO, Virginia Association OF Realtors

"The Swanepoel Trends Report is 'the' go-to book on what is happening within the industry, a great source of real information to help brokers and brands plan for what lies ahead. I have been a subscriber since inception. It gets better and better every year."

Sherry Chris, President & CEO, Better Homes and Gardens Real Estate

"Love how the Swanepoel Trends Report explains difficult concepts and plots out complex issues on grids, so it's easy to grasp and understand."

Simon Chen, CEO, ERA

"The Swanepoel Trends Report and the T3 Summit always deliver. They provide important and insightful analysis about the trends, people and companies in the real estate business."

Ryan O'Hara, CEO, Move, Inc.

"Every month during our Executive Strategy Group Meeting, our executive team selects one trend from the Swanepoel Trends Report to talk through. We discuss this trend and identify a positive opportunity we want to pursue in response to the trend, keeping us ahead of the curve."

Lennox Scott, CEO, John L Scott

"The Swanepoel Trends Report is always one of my 'go to' reference guides regarding future trends in the real estate vertical. Truly a phenomenal resource and one that provides great insight and value."

Bob Goldberg, CEO, National Association of Realtors

"The Swanepoel Trends Report is our barometer for making sure we are not missing anything."

Merri Jo Cowan, CEO, MFRMLS

"We find that The Swanepoel Trends Report does identify and validate those issues and opportunities we all need to address and pay attention to as we plan our respective futures."

Pat Riley, CEO, Allen Tate

"The Swanepoel Trends Report is a trusted source for me and our firm."

Jeff Detwiler, CEO, Long and Foster

"The Swanepoel Trends Report is the one annual publication that I have purchased for myself and our leadership team since BoomTown's inception. The report is always packed with valuable insights that help inform our strategy."

Grier Allen, CEO, BoomTown

"Because we know the Swanepoel Trends Report comes out annually, it has become our annual reality check."

Tom Phillips, CEO, Bright MLS

2019 Swanepoel Trends Report

14th Annual Edition

T3 Sixty   Enabling Intelligent Change

Swanepoel Trends Report

Silver medalist for best business reference, AXIOM Business Book Awards

Editorial Team

Editor-in-Chief
Stefan Swanepoel

Executive Editor
Paul Hagey

Managing Editor
Tinus Swanepoel

Technology Editor
Jack Miller

Staff Writers
Travis Saxton, Kevin McQueen,
Thomas Mitchell, Michele Conn,
Dean Cottrill, Clint Skutchan

Guest Contributors
Matt Cohen, Mark Lesswing,
Joseph Rand, Jeremy Conaway,
Sam DeBord and Ben Clark

Design
Tinus Swanepoel, Jennifer Tumala

Editorial Assistant
Karen Smith

Published by RealSure, Inc and T3 Sixty, LLC
29122 Rancho Viejo Rd, Suite 102
San Juan Capistrano, CA 92675
949.627.8877

t360.com

ISBN 978-0-9863779-6-9
Price $199.95 USA
Printed in the United States of America

Copyright © 2019 by RealSure, Inc.
All rights reserved.

Except as permitted under the United States Copyright Act of 1976, no part of this publication may be reproduced or distributed in any form or by any means or stored in a database or retrieval system without the prior written permission of the publisher. Images may be protected by copyright and should not be used without approval.

Most of the companies mentioned in this report own numerous trademarks and other marks. This report, the publishers, the author, the contributors or any other party involved in this Report in any way, will not seek to challenge or dilute any of these marks. Specifically, Realtor is a registered trademark of the National Association of Realtors.

Limit of Liability/Disclaimer of Warranty:

While the publisher, authors, contributors and editors have used their best efforts to present neutral, accurate, and reasonable views of the industry and its participants, they make no representation or warranties with respect to the accuracy or completeness of the contents of each publication and specifically disclaim any implied warranties.

T3 Sixty serves many companies and organizations stated in this report as a management consulting firm and may also, from time to time, be an investor in some of the companies mentioned in this report. However, no confidential information or information covered by a nondisclosure agreement was used.

References to companies, products and services also do not constitute or imply endorsement, and neither is any reference or absence of reference intended to harm, advantage or disadvantage a company or person. The publishers, editorial team and T3 Sixty shall not be liable for any loss or any other commercial damages, including but not limited to special, incidental, consequential or other damages.

Images and photos not of a specific-named person or available under creative commons was purchased through Shutterstock and may be protected by copyright.

Publications

As of January 2019

2018	Swanepoel Trends Report (2019)
	Important MLS Issues Answered
	Swanepoel Mega 1000
	Swanepoel Trends Report (2018)
	Swanepoel Power 200
2017	MLS 2020 Agenda
	Commercial Real Estate ALERT
	Finding New Clarity
	Winning on the Web
	Swanepoel Trends Report
	Swanepoel Power 200
2016	Homeowner Insights
	Digitization of the Home Buying Process
	DANGER Report Canada
	Swanepoel Trends Report
	Swanepoel Power 200
2015	T3 Risk Guide
	DANGER Report USA
	T3 Tech Guide
	Swanepoel Trends Report
	Swanepoel Power 200
2014	Real Estate Confronts Agent Reviews
	Swanepoel Trends Report
	Swanepoel Power 200
2013	Swanepoel Technology Report
	Swanepoel Trends Report
2012	Swanepoel Trends Report
2011	Swanepoel Trends Report
2010	Swanepoel Trends Report
	Swanepoel Social Media Report
1997–2009	Swanepoel Trends Report (2009, 2008, 2007, 2006)
	Real Estate Confronts Goal Setting vs. Business Planning (2005)
	Real Estate Confronts Bundled Services (2005)
	Real Estate Confronts Customer Acquisition (2004)
	Real Estate Confronts the Future (2004)
	Real Estate Confronts Profitability (2003)
	Real Estate Confronts the Banks (2002)
	Real Estate Confronts the e-Consumer (2000)
	Real Estate Confronts Technology (1999)
	Real Estate Confronts Reality (1997)

Table of Contents

x   **Foreword**
by Helen, Hoddy and Hoby Hanna

xii   **Preface**
by Stefan Swanepoel

14   **Trend 10: The Residential Real Estate Brokerage Shift**

Suddenly Arrived in 2018
by Stefan Swanepoel

30   **Trend 09: The Evolving Real Estate Value Proposition**

Redesigning the Brokerage Relationships with Agents and Consumers
by Joe Rand and Stefan Swanepoel

48   **Trend 08: Blockchain + Real Estate**

Cryptocurrency, Fractional Ownership and Optimized Real Estate Processes
by Mark Lesswing and Paul Hagey

62   **Trend 07: The Digital End-To-End Real Estate Transaction Dream**

Closer than Ever, But Still Far Away
by Ben Clark and Jeremy Conaway

From the Frontlines

The industry is at an inflection point, forcing the traditional brokerage business model to evolve. We reached out to five leaders — Real Estate One Co-President Dan Elsea, BHHS Fox & Roach Realtors President Joan Docktor, Windermere Real Estate Managing Principal OB Jacobi, William Pitt-Julia B. Fee Sotheby's International Realty President and Owner Paul Breunich, and William Raveis Real Estate Co-President Chris Raveis — to get their insights and thoughts on the changing industry and how they are preparing for, and responding to, the change.

82 Trend 06: The NAR - Broker Relationship

How Brokerages Can Best Leverage NAR
by Sam DeBord

102 Trend 05: Real Estate Data Standards

What's Really Happening with RETS and Web API?
by Kevin McQueen and Jack Miller

116 Trend 04: Understanding the Housing Supply Crisis

Why Rising Inventory Levels Will Likely Remain Low
by Lawrence Yun

134 Trend 03: The Brokerage Technology Conundrum

How to Develop a Smart Tech Strategy
by Travis Saxton and Jack Miller

154 Trend 02: The Future of Real Estate Artificial Intelligence

Voice-Activated Search, Virtual Assistants and Optimized Lead Conversion
by Matt Cohen and Paul Hagey

178 Trend 01: Mapping the New Residential Real Estate Brokerage Landscape

A Comparison of the Industry's Predominant Business Models
by Stefan Swanepoel and Paul Hagey

Foreword

Helen Hanna Casey
Chief Executive Officer
Howard Hanna Real Estate Services

Howard W. "Hoddy" Hanna, III
Chairman
Hanna Holdings, Inc.

Today's real estate business is not for alarmists, pessimists or quitters. The battle for sales is intense. With smarter, tech-savvy consumers and powerful, new competitors, we need to boldly adapt, create and innovate. Throughout our industry's history, change has been a constant. Disruptors and new models have emerged in every era.

How we adapt to change is what is important. To be successful, we must embrace, accept and meet the opportunities in front of us. We must be innovators and create our destiny. It is all about finding the best way to improve the real estate experience for our agents and clients.

Technology is still a foreign word for too many, but it will continue to advance, and we must invest in it to meet the future. So many brokers consider it a negative force and do not see the incredible opportunities it provides. Technology is not the competition, and fear holds many of us back.

Artificial intelligence (AI) and data management are fast becoming the industry's focus. AI is a great tool to bring buyers and agents together — it can generate a lead and match a buyer with a property. It will also enable us to respond better to consumer needs and to be more strategic and responsive in real time, or possibly, even before a seller or buyer knows they want to transact. However, its true value will be in the client relationships it helps foster.

However, technology and data will only go so far. After a lead is created, agents' skill and knowledge must take over. Agents take buyers to tour properties, and negotiate on their behalf. Consumers demand high touch, but also want high tech. We have a responsibility to give our agents the tools to meet consumer demand.

Agents need data-driven solutions that require less of their time and help them build their business. They can then focus on their clients, positioning themselves as the local expert and providing great customer service. This is an era of instant gratification for our agents as well as our consumers.

Howard W. "Hoby" Hanna, IV
President
Howard Hanna Real Estate
Brokerage

We all must be on a mission to deliver top-notch consumer experience — this is the starting point for everything. Both brokers and agents need to deliver consistent results and an experience that cannot be found down the street. Marketing will always drive our business. Today, marketing and technology are often synonymous with each other. Marketing costs will not go down, but these dollars will be distributed differently. There are more channels than ever before, and we need to ensure that we and our agents use the most effective ones available.

Brokers must continue to develop and implement tools and systems that make the real estate process easier and more convenient, while also delivering the value consumers expect from their broker and agent. Brokerage websites and portals list what is for sale, but agents provide the knowledge.

Our future is not possible without careful strategic planning, and now, a thorough implementation of technology, and that is why the *Swanepoel Trends Report* is so important to us — it provides insights into what is happening and what to do about it.

Change is upon us, the challenges are great and competition is fierce, but a watchful eye and bold action will give us an opportunity to achieve success. It starts today, every day.

Howard W. "Hoddy" Hanna, III
Chairman, Hanna Holdings, Inc.

Helen Hanna Casey
CEO, Howard Hanna Real Estate Services

Howard W. "Hoby" Hanna, IV
President, Howard Hanna Real Estate Brokerage

Preface

We have written about trends, innovation, technology and change for decades. We have fairly consistently and accurately identified where the industry would land before it touched the ground.

This understanding comes from deeply dissecting and analyzing new business models and trends. Over the last few years, we have watched and chronicled the gradual transforming pressure now rocking the industry to its core. After years of gradual build up, big change is suddenly upon us.

The industry is already far down the path of this significant shift, which we believe will be the single largest industry transformation in living memory. A shift larger than the Century 21 franchise explosion of the seventies, the Re/Max revolution of eighties or the Keller Williams Realty surge of the 2000s.

The latest shift will fundamentally change many key residential real estate brokerage business components: broker-agent relationships, brokerage-consumer relationships, the brokerage value proposition, commission and compensation structures, brokerage profitability, brokerage valuations, the brokerage business model and more.

In chapter 10, we outline the reengineering taking place, the context behind the shifting ground under brokers' feet. We explain the innovation cycles that have shaped the industry through history, their pattern, their impact and how they influenced the industry.

This cycle, Stage 9, is fueled by outside capital and is moving at a momentum the industry has not experienced before. Major, new players and models have already emerged fully committed to changing the real estate transaction, as well as the industry's leaderboard.

There is so much noise. Seemingly, every day a major development rocks the industry, often larger than the one we have barely digested.

These are exciting times. These are scary times. These are confusing times. This is the time to act!

Everyone is hungry for stability, for more analysis and more clarity. In these turbulent times, we at T3 Sixty will attempting to clarify and address those needs. That has always been, and will always be, our commitment to our industry.

On behalf of the T3 Sixty team,

Stefan Swanepoel
New York Times and Wall Street Journal Best-Selling Author,
Editor-in-Chief of the Swanepoel Trends Report
Chairman and CEO, T3 Sixty
November 2018

10 The Residential Real Estate Brokerage Shift

Suddenly Arrived in 2018

The residential real estate brokerage industry is facing a significant shift. A slew of new models and billions of dollars of outside investment challenge the dominant residential real estate brokerage model that emerged during the sixties and seventies – when many of today's major independents formed, and franchising began. Substantial change is afoot and most brokers can feel it. But this period of transformation is not unique. The industry has experienced similar cataclysms throughout its history.

In this chapter, T3 Sixty chronicles the current shift in the context of the industry's long history of innovation and change.

Patterns

Almost daily, news emerges about a new model, millions of new funding, or a huge acquisition. This cultivates discomfort and fear, and also competitiveness — normal emotions when dealing with massive change.

Change typically occurs at a relatively constant pace and at regular intervals. However, some periods experience more dynamic change than others. The industry is in one of those times now.

After three years of research, T3 Sixty recently completed a book documenting the residential real estate brokerage industry's journey from a fledgling, 150 years ago, to the behemoth it is today.

This book, titled *Real Estate DNA: The history of the residential real estate brokerage industry*, provides a year-by-year account of the specific events that shaped the industry into what it is today. It provides unparalleled insight into important industry-changing decisions, but is a separate 120-page read.

From that extensive research, T3 Sixty has distilled more than just the industry's history. Repeating patterns revealed themselves; these cycles occurred at fairly consistent intervals.

The Real Estate Industry Innovation Cycle

A study published in the Harvard Business Review in 2002 outlined a maturation curve. Based on the study of 1,345 large mergers completed over a thirteen-year period, it showed four stages of maturation (or consolidation as the study put it): Opening, Scale, Focus and Balance.

T3 Sixty found that the residential real estate brokerage industry follows a similar cycle. The section below outlines the industry's past as well as where the industry currently finds itself.

Although no examination leads to perfect predictions, it does provide a better understanding of where things are headed and why.

Understanding the industry's innovation cycle and the characteristics of each stage will help real estate leaders develop smarter strategies as this industry cycle crests and the seeds of the next emerge.

> "Residential real estate brokerage remains a place where millionaires can pop up like weeds with sheer determination and good old street hustle."
>
> Stefan Swanepoel

Ignoring the Shift

Ignoring or failing to see a significant shift clearly can have dire impacts. Some of the companies and leaders below learned the hard way. These companies all showcase the costs of failing to innovate when an industry faces significant changes, just where the real estate brokerage industry is today.

Palm
In 2000, Palm, maker of the first personal digital assistant (PDA) successfully marketed worldwide had a valuation of $53 billion. It clung to old technology and did not adapt to the next cycle of innovation. Hewlett-Packard bought it for $1.2 billion less than a decade later in 2010, and discontinued it the following year.

Blockbuster
In 2000, Blockbuster passed on an opportunity to acquire Netflix for $50 million and decided to maintain focus on its brick-and-mortar movie rental business model (it had 9,000 stores across the US in 2004). By March 2018, Blockbuster closed one of it last stores and saw a market cap of $5 billion wiped out within a decade. Meanwhile, Netflix exploded to a 2018 market cap of over $150 billion.

Yahoo
In 2006, Yahoo passed on acquiring Facebook for $1 billion. Facebook's market cap soared above $450 billion in 2018. Still sitting on 20 percent of the search engine market, Yahoo got another opportunity — this time to sell itself to Microsoft for $44.8 billion in 2008. Yahoo scuttled the deal, leading to a decade slide into 2017 when Verizon bought the struggling company for ten cents on the dollar, for $4.48 billion.

Blackberry
In 2010, BlackBerry was the second largest smartphone operating system in the world, with a 20 percent market share. Only behind the Symbian mobile operating system, BlackBerry's operating system was used by Samsung, Motorola, Sony Ericsson, and, above all, Nokia. By 2018, Symbian was gone and Blackberry dwindled to less than 0.1 percent market share.

> "What I can't figure out is why Steve Jobs is even trying to be the CEO of Apple? He knows he can't win."
> Former Microsoft CEO Bill Gates (1998)

> "Google is not a real company. It's a house of cards."
> Steve Ballmer, CEO, Microsoft (2004)

> "Neither Redbox nor Netflix are even on the radar screen in terms of competition."
> Former Blockbuster CEO Jim Keyes (2008)

Residential Real Estate Brokerage Stages

To chronologize the history of the Residential Real Estate Brokerage—*Real Estate DNA*—we researched and analyzed the major events, innovations, acquisitions and shifts that impacted the industry over the past one-and-a-half centuries.

Examination of the past hundred years (Stages 3-9 below) revealed that industry innovation cycles have occurred approximately every 13-18 years as follows:

Brokerage Stages	Years	Span
Stage 1 – The Early Years	Pre 1870	N/A
Stage 2 – The Second Industrial Rev.	1871 – 1914	N/A
Stage 3 – Roaring Twenties	1915 – 1928	13 years
Stage 4 – The Depression and WW II	1929 – 1945	16 years
Stage 5 – Baby Boom Generation	1946 – 1964	18 years
Stage 6 – Franchising Expansion	1965 – 1979	14 years
Stage 7 – Corporate America	1980 – 1995	15 years
Stage 8 – The Internet	1996 – 2011	15 years
Stage 9 – Capital Infusion	2012 –	

Stage 5 – Baby Boom Generation

Stage 6 – Franchising Expansion

Stage 7 – Corpora

Stage 9 Capital Infusion

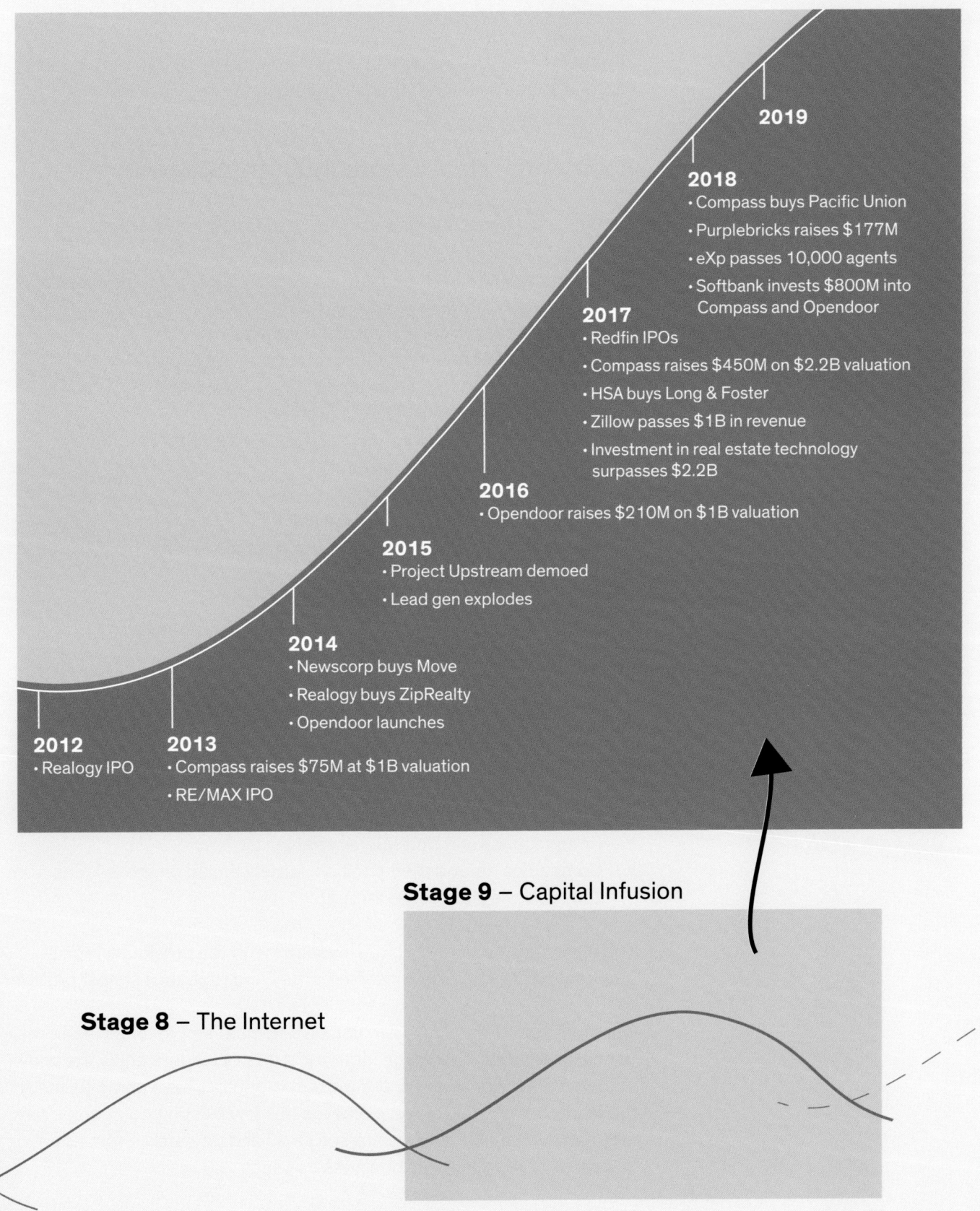

2019

2018
- Compass buys Pacific Union
- Purplebricks raises $177M
- eXp passes 10,000 agents
- Softbank invests $800M into Compass and Opendoor

2017
- Redfin IPOs
- Compass raises $450M on $2.2B valuation
- HSA buys Long & Foster
- Zillow passes $1B in revenue
- Investment in real estate technology surpasses $2.2B

2016
- Opendoor raises $210M on $1B valuation

2015
- Project Upstream demoed
- Lead gen explodes

2014
- Newscorp buys Move
- Realogy buys ZipRealty
- Opendoor launches

2013
- Compass raises $75M at $1B valuation
- RE/MAX IPO

2012
- Realogy IPO

Stage 9 – Capital Infusion

Stage 8 – The Internet

Source: T3 Sixty

Real Estate Industry Stages

The real estate brokerage industry innovation cycle can be organized into quadrants, similar to those outlined in the Harvard Business Review study.

Residential Real Estate Industry Stage Quadrants

Each quartile has a few primary characteristics, listed below:

Quadrant 1: Birth (3-5 years)
- Birth of new models or concepts.
- New competitors of incumbents emerge.
- New enduring business models become apparent.
- Deregulation or rule changes occur.

Quadrant 2: Build (3-5 years)
- Newer models go mainstream.
- Newer companies build scale.
- Consolidations and acquisitions pick up.
- Newer models and incumbents race for leadership position.

Quadrant 3: Growth (3-5 years)
- Newer models change the industry, incumbents respond.
- Newer models focus on growing market share.
- Mega deals occur.
- Final stage winners emerge.

Quadrant 4: Domination (3-5 years)
- The titans reign.
- Leaders ride the crest of the top wave.
- Complacency and bureaucracy set in.
- Companies defend their position, largely based on the lessons from the cycle they just came through.

The next stage's quadrant No. 1 overlaps with the previous stage's quadrant No. 4, and a new cycle emerges and repeats a similar pattern.

Quadrants No. 1 and No. 4 are usually the most stable times in the residential real estate brokerage industry. Industry leaders enjoy the spoils of their market domination, and most competitors have come to accept the leaderboard. New models emerge but few existing companies pay attention as the new models are still small and untested. From approximately six to ten years it is business as usual.

The crazy times — the times filled with fear, excitement and big moves, predominantly occur during quadrants No. 2 and No. 3. In these times, newer models gain unexpected traction, and the game starts to change for large portions of the market. This is where the industry finds itself today, in the years 2018-2019: Stage 9 appears to be moving from quadrant No. 2 to quadrant No. 3 right now.

This gradual-then-sudden pattern of change is part of the industry's natural evolution. For companies to successfully navigate each cycle and survive requires bold, innovative and educated action.

The Drivers of Change

Every stage has primary and secondary key drivers, which catalyze significant industry-changing events, and a cadre of new players that emerge.

A few examples of new dominant leaders created during previous stages include:

- **Stage 6 (Franchising Expansion):** Century 21 and Re/Max were founded and among the first companies to use franchising to expand nationally (later globally).

- **Stage 7 (Corporate America):** The nation's top four companies were all acquired and additional expansion created giants such as Coldwell Banker.

- **Stage 8 (The Internet):** Realtor.com, Zillow, and Trulia pioneered a portal craze still flourishing today.

Stage 9, fueled by enormous amounts of capital and a vision to reinvent the industry, has seen new powerful players emerge including Redfin, Compass, eXp Realty and Purplebricks. Redfin and Compass have already landed on the Top 10 leaderboard, while the others are poised to land there within the next few years.

Driver 1 - Capital

The influx of huge amounts of outside capital has fueled companies who, under normal financing scenarios, may not have survived or would not have grown nearly as fast. Given the time-warping character of large amounts of cash, Stage 9 could be on a shorter timeline relative to previous industry stages.

A decade or two ago, venture capital investors tended to cap startup funding at approximately $50 million before requiring the company to make a profit. Then, Amazon came along and changed that paradigm.

What Could $15 Billion Buy You Today?

The value of a public companies were based on their market capitalization as at time of publication. Companies that recently raised money were valued at the most recent funding round. The valuation of private companies were determined by using recent private sales and estimating a fair market value based on comparable data. Note that companies mentioned in this chart are not for sale and the chart was compiled simply to illustrate the huge difference between "new business model" and "traditional business model" companies.

OPTION 1

Zillow

Compass

Opendoor

Redfin

eXp Realty

OR

OPTION 2

Realogy
Including: Coldwell Banker, Century 21, Sotheby's, ERA, BH&G, NRT, Corocan, ZipRealty, Climb Realty

Re/Max

Keller Williams Realty

Berkshire Hathaway HomeServices
Including: Edina, EWM, FirstWeber, Gloria Nilson, Harry Norman, CBS Home, Houlihan Lawrence, Huff Realty, Intero, Kentwood, IOWA, Long & Foster, Long Realty, Realty South, Reece Nichols, Roberts, WR Realtors, Semonin, Wood Bros

Independent Brokerages
Including: Alain Pinel Realtors, Baird & Warner, Crye-Leike, Daniel Gale, Douglas Elliman, FC Tucker, First Team, Howard Hanna, John L Scott, John R Wood, Latter & Blum, Lyon Real Estate, Michael Saunders, NP Dodge, Sibcy Cline, The Keyes Company, Watson Realty, William Raveis, Windermere, @Properties

Source: T3 Sixty

The retail and e-commerce giant, founded in 1994, raised $2.1 billion before breaking even, let alone returning a profit.

This altered the philosophy of startup funding and growth. It opened the door for startups to pursue immediate growth at all costs with a goal of achieving market dominance and profits only in the long term. The cast here is well-known: Facebook, Twitter, Tesla and Uber. Capital at this scale changes the rulebook that has typically governed business growth.

For example, in 2016, Amazon leased a fleet of forty Boeing cargo planes, and in 2017 committed $1.5 billion to build Prime Air. So today, the tech behemoth who made its name as a retailer is the owner of one of the world's largest plane fleets. Walmart never had planes. Walmart never needed planes. Why would retailers need planes when they had stores?

A similar change is happening in the real estate industry. Investors are pouring billions into the real estate tech industry. In 2018 alone (through the third quarter), investors have made over $1.9 billion in investments in real estate startups, including $725 million in Opendoor and $400 million in Compass.

Brokerages never had to compete with so many different companies with access to so much capital and no near-term need for balance sheets that come up black. For more discussion on the vast influence and impact of outside capital on residential real estate, see the *2018 Swanepoel Trends Report* top trend, "Follow the Money," and the update on page 172.

Driver 2 - Technology

Beyond capital, technology has also flooded the residential real estate brokerage industry with game-changing innovation, which is gradually transforming the way consumers buy, sell, rent and manage homes, and the way brokerages operate.

The efficiencies, scale and data made possible by today's technology allows firms to automate processes, centralize services, make better, more informed decisions and provide better service to their agents and consumers than ever before.

In many cases, newer companies can better leverage modern technology than existing companies because they are built from the ground up with it. New business models do not have the disadvantage of legacy systems tailored for a previous era. For a detailed review of the modern brokerage industry technology landscape, see Trend No. 3 in this year's *Swanepoel Trends Report*.

In short, technology and the scalability, efficiency and data-powered operations it enables is no longer a broker supplement but has moved to center stage and become the core brokerage feature.

This shift enables new companies to gain disproportionately large valuations compared to their traditional counterparts. For example, the five companies Zillow Group, Redfin, Compass, Opendoor and eXp Realty collectively have a greater valuation than the industry's largest brokerages and franchisors combined, including Coldwell Banker, Century 21, Sotheby's Realty International, ERA Real Estate, Better Homes and Gardens, Re/Max, Keller Williams, Berkshire Hathaway HomeServices and the nation's largest twenty independent brokerages.

Remember that a big portion of a startup's valuation typically centers on the promise of future growth and profits based on an upward trajectory. Their high valuations reflect investors' bets that the new companies will take an industry by storm and achieve great scale. If they make an industry splash, investors collect a large payout. If they fizzle, they become a historical blip, a bet that simply did not pan out.

Current industry leaders have large market shares and significant revenue and profits, but will they have it in a decade from now? Judging by previous industry stages and innovation cycles, a number of players on the current leaderboard will disappear.

Driver 3 - Velocity

The speed at which products, platforms and entire new businesses gain wide adoption is speeding up. Although not exactly comparable, the speed it took certain technologies to reach 50 million users provides an example. It took the telephone seventy-five years, TV thirteen years, the internet four years, and took Angry Birds thirty-five days! The importance of these innovations vary greatly, but the point remains — the speed with which new platforms go from zero to hero has shrunk immensely.

It took long-standing real estate powerbrokers Weichert Realtors, Long & Foster, Howard Hanna Real Estate, Douglas Elliman and William Raveis Real Estate between forty and sixty years to reach $10 billion in annual sales.

Newcomers Redfin, Realty One Group and HomeSmart achieved the same annual sales volume in just a little more than a decade. Compass has bought and marketed itself to the nation's third largest brokerage with an annual sales volume of $14 billion in just five years (or 28 billion if one includes the Pacific Union acquisition).

The inaugural *Swanepoel Mega 1000* (mega1000.com), which ranks the nation's thousand largest brokerages by sales volume, clearly reveals the industry shift. Four of the country's twelve largest brokerages in 2017 were less than two decades old — Redfin (No. 4, fifteen years old), Realty One Group (No. 7, fourteen years old), Compass (No. 9, six years old) and HomeSmart (No. 11, nineteen years old).

Startups wield speed as one of their competitive advantages, and in 2019 they have the money to scale fast.

Where Are We Now?
With Stage 9 starting in 2012, the industry is rapidly approaching the midpoint of this cycle, which means Quadrant 3 activities will dominate the next few years.

Quadrant 3 activities include:
- The industry feels change brought by new business models and incumbents respond.
- Newer models quickly grow market share.
- Mega deals take place — large companies purchase other large companies.
- The final stage winners emerge and begin solidifying their position.

All industry stages differ, of course, and do not follow the same beats or timeframes. However, a century of data strongly suggests that well-funded and innovative Stage 9 is in full swing and will begin to crest in the early 2020s.

Existing Players Fight Back
Industry leadership boards constantly change. For example, only a decade ago, the nation's five largest companies were Exxon, GE, Microsoft, Citigroup and Bank of America, but today, the leaderboard includes Alphabet, Apple, Microsoft, Amazon and Facebook.

What a difference ten years makes!

The last few years reveal that the real estate leaderboard is also in flux. Real estate has not seen a new leader in over two decades. Both NRT and HomeServices of America have been the industry's largest two brokerages since they emerged approximately twenty years ago. They still hold a wide lead in 2019. Although the *Swanepoel Mega 1000* will not announce 2019's largest brokerages until May, T3 Sixty anticipates that Compass and Redfin will both be in the top five and eXp Realty in the top 10.

Many existing players (both leading industry franchisors and brokerages) are not lying down. Many are vigorously competing to protect their

> "Startups wield speed as one of their competitive advantages, and in 2019 they have the money to scale fast."

market share and brands, and have made major moves in recent years. The brokerage leader profiles in this report make that abundantly clear. For example, legacy players have recently made some big moves:

- The largest holding company in residential real estate brokerage, Realogy, acquired ZipRealty for $166 million in 2014. The firm rebranded it as ZapLabs (zaplabs.com), which has yet to deliver a noticeable impact. In 2018, it also announced that it would launch a Direct Buyer model, starting with its Coldwell Banker brand.

- In 2017, Keller Williams Realty began describing itself as a tech company and pledged to invest $1 billion to make that a reality. In 2018, it launched its voice-activated virtual assistant Kelle. It, too, announced a Direct Buyer play in 2018.

- In 2018, Re/Max acquired well-regarded real estate platform booj (booj.com) to provide better tech to its franchisees.

On the consolidation side, recent acquisitions by legacy brokerages include:

- In 2017, HomeServices of America, the nation's second largest brokerage, bought Long & Foster, the nation's third largest brokerage.

- In 2018, Alain Pinel, the nation's 10th largest brokerage, acquired San Francisco Bay Area boutique firm, Hill & Co.

- In 2018, Howard Hanna Real Estate, the nation's sixth largest brokerage, acquired Allen Tate Real Estate, the nation's 27th largest brokerage.

Things are moving fast.

Takeaway

Shifts are nothing new for the residential real estate brokerage industry. When Century 21 popularized franchising in residential real estate in the early seventies, its network grew to 3,300 franchises in just six years. That was a big shift.

By introducing the 100 percent compensation model and luring top producers in the seventies, Re/Max grew into the world's largest real estate franchise company. That was a big shift.

> "Hubris so often plays a big role in leaderboard shake-ups, but it is not the only driver. Each innovation cycle sees the game shift — status quo operations do not quite fit the new eras."

Realogy-precursors HSF and Cendant began rolling up multiple real estate brands under one holding company and created the real estate's first multi-brand conglomerate in the late nineties. That was a big shift.

When the Keller Williams Realty model, with its infectious culture and profit-sharing, caught fire in the 2000s and became the world's largest real estate company by agent count, that was a big shift.

These companies were all once the disruptors (in Stages 6, 7 and 8).

Now they are incumbents fighting to protect their market share against Stage 9 newcomers. T3 Sixty estimates Stage 9 began approximately in 2012, give or take a year or two.

The industry was climbing out of the housing crisis at that time. Technology had been around more than a decade and was maturing quickly.

New models had already launched but were still untested and struggling to gain traction. Existing players had survived the downturn and were giving themselves survival pats on the back. Many leaders did not see the powerful newcomers coming.

Lead Contributor:

Stefan Swanepoel
Stefan, Chairman and CEO of T3 Sixty, is widely recognized as the leading visionary on real estate trends. With over 35 years of experience in the real estate industry, he served as CEO of nine companies and two nonprofit organizations. He has authored or co-authored over forty books including the *Swanepoel Trends Report*, *Swanepoel Power 200* and *Swanepoel Mega 1000*. Stefan can be reached at stefan@t360.com.

09 The Evolving Real Estate Value Proposition

Redesigning the Brokerage Relationships with Agents and Consumers

The relationships brokers have with agents and consumers is not simple. Many brokers support independent contractor agents with organizational structure, insurance, technology, marketing, legal guidance and contractual help. They also form relationships with consumers through their brands. New brokerage business models are fundamentally redefining these relationships, especially with consumers.

This chapter chronicles how and why the broker value proposition with agents and with consumers has changed and proposes ways for brokerages to improve it. Readers should review the preceding chapter, Trend No. 10, "The Residential Real Estate Brokerage Inflection Point" before diving into this one.

The Changing Broker-Agent Relationship

As technology reshapes the residential real estate brokerage industry, the traditional brokerage value propositions for both agents and consumers have changed. Firms with newer business models are also forging different relationships with agents and consumers, which contributes to the relationship shifts.

The Evolving Compensation Model

The broker-agent relationship has steadily evolved from what is known today as the traditional brokerage model, which emerged after the second World War. Many brokerages from that baby boom era were founded and led by pillar-of-the-community brokers. They hung their shingles on Main Street and built brokerage firms around their individual talents and personalities, which eventually made them rainmakers for their brokerage and agents.

These brokers' value proposition to agents was simple. They provided their agents leads and then supported them with systems, infrastructure, marketing and culture. In exchange, agents worked with buyers and sellers and guided transactions to a close. As partners, brokers and agents shared transaction commissions in what became known as the 50-50 split. In this system, brokers and agents worked together, much as a modern real estate team does, with brokers leading the way in most aspects of the business and agents falling in line.

Many brokerages founded during this stage carried the names of their founding broker, reflecting the central role the founding personalities played in the business. Examples include Nothnagle Realtors (1948), Howard Hanna Real Estate (1957) and Allen Tate Realtors (1957).

The franchising and national expansion boom in the industry's next era, Stage 6: 1965-1979, shifted the traditional brokerage from a local focal point to a national one (for a full discussion of industry stages, see Trend No. 10). The era introduced both a national and, decades later, a global scope for real estate company brands and networks. Gradually, the ability of local rainmaker brokers to generate the bulk of their agents' leads began to decline as national marketing campaigns and national brands started generating leads as well. In-company referrals became more prominent as these companies greatly expanded their footprints.

Brokers progressively took on more agents, shifting their focus more

> "The real estate broker is the last commission-driven outpost of American entrepreneurship."
>
> Stefan Swanepoel

to management, contractual oversight, brand consistency, training and coaching and managing new technologies. Agents, now part of these larger firms, were increasingly left to generate more business themselves.

New models emerged that offered agents 100 percent of the commission (such as Realty Executives and Re/Max) for a monthly predetermined, fixed management fee in lieu of splitting commissions.

This dramatically changed the traditional relationship between brokers and agents. In the seventies, when the 100 percent commission model launched, most real estate brokerages were offering agents 50-50 commission splits. The new models forced them to adapt. They began introducing a sliding commission-split scale to agents, such as 70-30 and 80-20 splits in favor of the agent, which dramatically reduced broker profitability. With a drop in profits came a reduction in services, which increasingly strained the broker-agent relationship, making agents more independent than before.

The next major shift in this broker-agent relationship occurred when new models (such as that employed by Keller Williams Realty) began capping the annual commissions agents had to share with their broker. This again pushed broker margins down, which led to significantly larger offices that could maximize profits with economies of scale. Standard traditional brokerages, which typically had 20 to 100 agents, began to grow many multiples larger. More brokerages today grow to as many as 400 to 1,000 agents.

Then, a cadre of brokers created a hybrid of the capped fee model and the management fee, introducing what today is referred to as the agent flat fee brokerage model in which agents pay a flat monthly fee and, in some cases, a per-transaction flat fee and no commissions. Firms with this model include HomeSmart, Realty One Group and United Real Estate. For a detailed analysis of this model, see Trend No. 3 in the *2017 Swanepoel Trends Report Trend*, "Agent Flat-Fee Brokerages on the Rise."

Each of these developments pushed the broker-agent dynamic from a more partnership relationship to more of a service provider relationship, where brokers increasingly provide a more limited, streamlined set of services. This sparked a resurgence of the team business model. For a detailed analysis of teams, see Trend No. 1 in the *2017 Swanepoel Trends Report*, "The Hypergrowth of Teams."

> "Firms with newer business models are also forging different relationships with consumers, which contributes to the relationship shifts."

The franchise model, the 100 percent commission concept, the capped company dollar model, the agent flat-fee model and the team model each changed the traditional broker value proposition. Real estate agents are more independent than they have ever been, paying for the services they use, from a variety of sources (their broker being just one), and customizing as much as they can.

Agents still need and can benefit from brokers but their growing independence has eroded the classic partnership value exchange. Brokers became service providers and now some brokers see themselves as part landlord, part technology vendor and part transaction coordinator.

Other Business Factors

Compensation changes signal one big way the broker-agent relationship has changed, but it is not the only one. The proliferation of powerful and relatively affordable technology over the past two decades has also changed the value real estate agents find from brokers. Other factors, covered below, have contributed as well.

Technology
Technology has impacted almost every facet of real estate, from consumer communication and acquisition to CRMs and contracts.

Whether through increased access to technology, more sophisticated vendors or more robust offerings, agents no longer must go to their brokers for many key services. Agents can now afford comparable systems on their own, with a wide variety of styles and price points.

That technology self-control significantly undermines brokers' ability to help agents with a part of their business they would highly value. More brokerages are building best-of-breed tech platforms that centralize popular, high-rated technology into one affordable, integrated system to reclaim this value exchange. They can often get better pricing, and build a better integrated system at scale, but it takes time, money and effort. See Trend No. 3 for an outline of how to implement a smart brokerage technology strategy.

Offices
The omnipresence of powerful mobile technology and high-speed cellular networks and internet connections allows agents to work from anywhere, including their home and the road.

Therefore, the need to come into an office to use a computer, to access the MLS, a fax machine or a phone are long gone. Agents now store and access files from a cloud server, sign contracts with e-signatures on platforms such as DocuSign and SkySlope, schedule and make appointments themselves, update listings on the MLS and place new ads on Facebook — all from their smartphone.

Offices are no longer a straightforward value that brokers can provide agents. Many brokers are building the virtual platforms that help agents better do their jobs on the go. Again, this takes a committed, smart tech strategy.

Marketing
Agents once needed brokers to facilitate marketing through newspaper advertising and postcard printing, which was burdensome for full-time agents to coordinate and often cheaper and easier at scale.

But with the rise of digital marketing and the ability to distribute listings to the MLS and popular portals with ease, most agents can market themselves and their listings to a greater degree than ever, without the help of a broker.

Training
Most licensing and almost all continuing education training today occurs online. Although numerous brokerages still offer some level of skills and productivity training, many agents serious about getting their career on the fast track hire coaches or third-party trainers who provide customized training, team and performance coaching for monthly or yearly fees.

Lead Generation
With the rise of powerful lead generation sites such as Zillow, realtor.com and Facebook, agents have an abundance of new-lead sources to choose from. With the responsibility of generating business now

mostly in agents' own hands, they are exploiting these new, sophisticated channels.

Of course, larger brokerages have an opportunity to build organized, streamlined lead generation strategies, which would benefit both their agents and their bottom line. These, too, require a smart, overarching tech strategy. Again, turn to Trend No. 3 in this report.

Agent Teams

Real estate agent teams have been an industry fixture for decades, but recently have proliferated and matured from an informal grouping, usually between friends and family, to larger more business-minded mini-companies.

> "Agents, and by proxy their brokers, held on to that gatekeeper role for far too long."

Teams are usually built around the skills of a top-producing agent — a rainmaker. Interestingly, these resemble the way pre-seventies rainmaker brokers operated, right down to the 50-50 commission split. Teams increase the relationship disconnect between brokers and agents. Team leaders tend to develop significantly stronger relationships with their team members than the broker does. The team leader provides the services traditionally associated with a broker — training, coaching, managing, feeding leads — and, often, purchases the technology platform upon which the team runs its business.

Team leaders, too, as a significant mini-real estate business have significant leverage with their brokers.

The Changing Consumer Value Proposition

Traditional brokers generally do not provide services directly to consumers; rather, they deliver value to consumers by empowering and supporting their agents in their consumer relationships — with oversight, systems, technology, facilities, training and other administrative tasks. Some of the ways brokers' relationships have changed with consumers are presented below.

Gatekeepers No Longer

At the peak of brokerages' consumer influence, consumers had to come to them and their agents to access houses for sale. This placed real estate brokers and agents in a gatekeeper role, which carried great power.

That gatekeeping role began to decline as listings began to become freely available online in the late nineties. Homebuyers no longer needed real estate professionals to access data about homes for sale — they could simply pull up a website and gain free access without having to form a relationship with a broker or agent.

A long hangover clouded brokers and agents' vision as that gatekeeper position began to wane. They did not quickly adapt when that value all-but-completely disappeared. Agents, and by proxy their brokers, held on to that gatekeeper role for far too long.

While brokers and agents' consumer-facing technology has improved, industry technology tends to lag behind what consumers want. For example, broker or agent websites generally do not provide an agent-client communication platform, collaboration, transaction management or regular status updates.

Newer business models seized upon this disconnect by focusing on building relationships directly with consumers and providing them powerful technology and new transacting opportunities, from discount brokers to the new Direct Buyers. These include Zillow, Redfin and Opendoor.

Of course, technology, while important and increasingly critical, is not the end-all-be-all. Brokerages and their agents provide immense value to consumers as empathic counselors, experienced stagers, negotiators and transaction experts.

Real Estate's Unique Two-Sided Marketplace

Real estate's unique two-sided marketplace is designed to provide consumers the best of two worlds. The system incentivizes cooperation among rival brokers and agents who compete to win listings but then cooperate on selling it. This collaboration, supported by the MLS system, allows homebuyers to work with any real estate agent or broker and generally gain access to every home for sale in a market.

Other industries do not enjoy that MLS-driven cooperation or share compensation as openly as real estate does. For example, car buyers

"Newer business models seized upon this disconnect by focusing on building relationships directly with consumers"

must go to every dealership in an area to price cars because dealers generally only sell the cars they have in inventory. In addition, car salespersons typically work for the dealer; in real estate, of course, agents represent consumer interests as a fiduciary.

New business models, including discount brokerages and Direct Buyers (also referred to as iBuyers), target the lack of consumer clarity about this two-sided real estate market benefit in their marketing, offering to provide rebates, discounts and other perks to consumers. This short-circuits the benefits for both buying and selling brokers in the two-sided marketplace. The market created by broker cooperation through a two-sided deal is an important but understated part of the traditional value proposition for brokers and agents, and consumers.

With the increasing prevalence of fee models such as discount brokerages and Direct Buyers that deviate from this established industry collaboration, the real estate brokerage industry should decide how it wants to make this value more clear to consumers.

If new models with alternative pricing strategies begin to take more market share, some traditional brokers may decide to shift how they cooperate with competitors. Some brokers propose that consumers pay a fee if they want to access the open real estate market, for example. The open system comes at a cost — new models have raised the question of who pays.

> "If new models with alternative pricing strategies begin to take more market share, some traditional brokers may decide to shift how they cooperate with competitors."

Ways to Strengthen the Brokerage Value Proposition

Brokerages have many options to improve their value propositions with their agents and consumers. Although many have begun implementing new strategies to varying degrees, a majority of brokers have a long way to go. Below is a suite of broad suggestions for brokerages to improve these relationships; they can be used as a checklist, as well as to provoke new ideas.

Develop Direct Consumer Relationships

Brokers should identify ways to provide more direct services to consumers, to compliment or supplement the work agents do. Brokers with independent contractor agents, of course, must do this in a way that does not step on their agents' toes.

This effort can have two-fold benefits. It can help agents provide a higher quality consumer experience, which will increase the value of the brokerage in agents' eyes. If branded and communicated clearly, it can also increase the brokerage's value in clients' eyes, too.

All brokers should explore, identify and invest in tools that can help their agents more efficiently serve their clients. They should perform this exercise at least twice each year. This applies to both brokers who have a more direct relationship with consumers and those that serve consumers primarily through their agents.

Indeed, Realogy and Keller Williams Realty announced Direct Buyer models in 2018, joining the ranks of relative newcomers Opendoor, Offerpad, RedfinNow and Zillow Offers. This service illustrates one way brokerages can support their agents with a direct consumer offering, and compete with newer models.

Become Better Rainmakers

Brokers should consider reasserting their role as a strong rainmaker for their agents. Digital and content marketing work, but take tremendous resources to do well, and, like newspaper advertising of old, is generally cheaper and easier to execute at scale.

In addition to adding the systems and strategies to generate more leads, brokerages should invest in technology and operations that deliver higher-quality leads more likely to transact to agents. These efforts can justify higher splits with agents.

Brokerages with affiliate businesses also have an opportunity to send agents leads from these divisions. For example, brokers with well-developed affiliate mortgage companies have often marketed those services to their agents for consumer referrals rather than vice-versa. These brokers can also fish upstream in that channel, and provide their agents valuable leads from a new source.

> "The popularity of virtual companies has demonstrated that large numbers of agents will trade office space for a more favorable compensation structure."

Reduce What Agents Do Not Value

Given that margins have declined, brokers need to find ways to do more with less, which means looking to dramatically cut fixed, large expenses. For example, brokers should change their perspective on the number and size of offices they have. The popularity of virtual companies has demonstrated that large numbers of agents will trade office space for a more favorable compensation structure.

Even agents who still want a physical presence do not need expensive retail space. Brokers that must have space should adopt the model now used by most service professional companies: less expensive (and less visible) office space in executive parks, where firms can house more agents at lower costs.

Develop Specialist Support Regions

Brokers should reassess the role of branch managers in their brokerages. Instead of promoting top sales agents or hiring good jack-of-all-trades managers to manage a single office, multi-office brokerages should cultivate a team of specialist managers skilled at multiple tasks ranging from recruiting, coaching, technology and more and have them oversee several offices.

Scale or Specialize

> "Middle-tier brokerages without standout brands will continue to feel the pressure ... "

Middle-tier brokerages are under the most pressure. Aside from a few outliers, they have only three options: specialize, scale or go home. Specialized brokerages are usually smaller and operate on the traditional rainmaker model, with the broker-owner doubling as a top producer or even a literal team leader. Even if they do not generate most of the leads, these firms tend to cultivate an elite, hyperlocal brand and culture with content and event marketing to match. These brokerages, with high per-agent productivity and a strong brand, can thrive as a local boutique.

Middle-tier brokerages without standout brands will continue to feel the pressure of higher agent splits and increased competition from discount brokerages. Brokerages not building strong, boutique brands need to get bigger, much bigger. These brokerages need to maximize their agent offerings by delivering quality leads and tools, and growing big enough to realize economies of scale and meaningful earnings.

Add Affiliated Businesses

Bigger brokerages need to diversify their income streams by developing affiliate services — mortgage, title, insurance, property

management – if they have not already done so. Many brokerages, of course, have done this for years.

Clients of these businesses overlap with brokerage operations. Brokers who can successfully transition clients from one homeservice to another can multiply the revenue and profit that the client brings to the firm, without taking anything away from agents. A well-run affiliate operation can add value to both agent and client relationships, if it focuses on improving the client experience as well as generating additional revenue.

Redefine Consumer Messaging

Brokers and agents need to reposition their value proposition to consumers. They should reduce their lowest-common-denominator services such as showing homes. Instead, they should emphasize their role as local experts, with intimate, street-by-street knowledge of the neighborhoods they serve. High-service brokers and agents should also highlight the additional array of services they offer, including pricing strategy, counseling, negotiation and transaction management.

Help Agents Expand Their Services

> "Real estate's two-sided marketplace is uniquely designed to provide consumers the best of two worlds."

Agents provide a range of valuable services to their clients but can go even further. Brokerages can help them find new, innovative ways to provide value and clear, compelling ways to message their value to consumers.

For example, agents have traditionally used third-party professionals for staging, but many homes do not require that level of preparation. Brokers can coach and train agents to take on more of this role themselves.

Encourage Agents to Get Buyer Agreements

Brokerages should encourage their agents to insist that buyers sign representation agreements. These agreements should make clear that a buyer agent's services deserve compensation, and designate a price that a buyer is expected to pay if the seller or seller's agent will not. Not only does this make the value buyer agents provide clear to buyers, but protects both brokers and agents from listings that offer little to no compensation to buyer's agents.

Takeaway

The brokerage value proposition to agents and consumers has changed immensely, since the modern real estate industry emerged after World War II. The industry, however, still clings to its historic gatekeeper role, and has done a poor job of articulating the full value of the modern real estate professional.

Technology plays a big role in these changes, in addition to newer business models that have slowly shifted the brokerage value proposition with agents and consumers over decades.

Brokerages must now reevaluate their offerings and the value they provide; if they do not adapt, they will become increasingly irrelevant.

Newer business models are also stressing real estate's two-sided marketplace, which has always been implicit, but now appears vulnerable. It exists because listing brokerages agree to split their commissions with buyer brokerages (through the MLS). Without the MLS, and without the compensation offered by the two-sided arrangement, the real estate market will be fundamentally different.

Relationships have always been the lifeblood of the residential real estate brokerage industry. 2018 is much different than it was half a century ago, and brokerages must reevaluate and revamp their value propositions – and better communicate them — to fit the modern needs of agents and consumers.

> "Relationships have always been the lifeblood of the residential real estate brokerage industry."

Lead Contributors:

Joseph Rand

Joseph is the author of *Disruptors, Discounters, and Doubters: A Guide for the Client-Oriented Future of the Real Estate Industry* published earlier this year. He also serves as Chief Creative Officer for Better Homes and Gardens Real Estate Rand Realty, one of the largest companies in the New York tristate region, with thirty offices and 1,000 agents who do over $2.5 billion in annual sales. Joseph can be reached at joseph.rand@randrealty.com.

Stefan Swanepoel

Stefan, Chairman and CEO of T3 Sixty, is widely recognized as the leading visionary on real estate trends. With over 35 years of experience in the real estate industry, he served as CEO of nine companies and two nonprofit organizations. He has authored or co-authored over forty books including the Swanepoel Trends Report, Swanepoel Power 200 and Swanepoel Mega 1000. Stefan can be reached at stefan@t360.com.

Mega 1000

Lookout for the 2019 Mega 1000 scheduled for release on Wednesday, May 1, 2019.

mega1000.com
t360.com

Dan Elsea, Co-President, Real Estate One

From the Frontlines

What are the chief industry changes that affect your brokerage today?

Longer-term, our consumer value proposition is changing. In our case, that centers on the speed of the transaction. Technology removes friction and transactions are becoming faster and easier to do. In the past, agents could rest on relationships – they really only had to fear another agent cold-calling one of their past clients. In today's world, with Zillow, Realtor dot com, Facebook and Google, and big data and artificial intelligence, agents face sophisticated competition every day. Sending a monthly newsletter just will not cut it now. To compete, agents must leverage technology and social media to develop deeper relationships with the consumers.

- **What are you doing about those changes?**

When we talk to our salespeople, we emphasize that they face a choice along a continuum. One side is the facilitator role, which centers on a task-based relationship with consumers, much of which can be automated and supported by technology. The other side is the personalized counselor who provides deep knowledge, expertise and support throughout a transaction.

Culturally, we focus on counseling over facilitation. Becoming a counselor takes work, study, and expertise. To help agents become better counselors, we are adapting training and coaching models. We emphasize that agents should defend their sphere of influence and force other agents to protect theirs. We currently operate under several brands and business models, all with a counseling focus. In the future, if the market dictates, we may introduce a new brand that centers on agents as facilitators.

We have also focused on developing, deep micro-market research, which we believe will be even more important going forward as it is expensive and difficult to scale, giving our agents an advantage over the general real estate portal market reports.

- **What are the biggest changes to your brokerage you have on the books for 2019? Why?**

We are large and a bit too decentralized now. We are centralizing more operations to provide more consistent service with higher-quality staff and coaching for our agents. We want to go beyond traditional coaching, which centers on accountability and systems, to a more holistic service with personal branding, marketing, technology and client-relationship coaching.

- **What keeps you up at night as a brokerage leader?**

Figuring out where the agent service mix will land. We are fairly certain that fees consumers pay will drift down because of efficiencies. We think that marketing homes will improve, and those costs will go down and the compensation brokerages pay to agents will go up.

We are not sure whether the eventual successful business model will look more like a branding company or a business management firm for agents, or a mixture of both. As a larger brokerage, we combine the two now, but we need to make sure we maintain the right balance.

- **How are you outperforming newer brokerage business models?**

We are constantly evolving our business model, we operate different models, some with intense marketing and branding support using a more traditional agent-compensation model and others with agent desk fees and a la carte services. For example, we have had a virtual brokerage offering for a decade. Our agents have physical offices they can use, but they pay a premium for that.

Much of our competition appears to come from discount brokers using a stripped-down service model, which attracts agents who lean toward the facilitation model, doing just a few transactions a year. We believe that technology-borne efficiencies will disproportionately affect lower-producing agents. We are working to develop win-win plans for top agents to compete effectively in an online, rarely-meet-client world.

The integration of our affiliated businesses — mortgage, title, casualty insurance, property management — into one transaction experience gives us a significant competitive edge. Our competition is just now realizing this integrated transaction experience enhances the consumer experience.

- **Where do you think newer models have an edge? What are you doing about them?**
That is hard to tell. Two developments have spawned new models — marketing efficiency and the shift in broker, agent value propositions. Technology has made marketing most properties – even multi-million dollar ones — incredibly efficient. Marketing a home may soon take two or three clicks and a text request to a good photographer.

Although technology forms the base for much of how we deliver our services, we do not see it as a long-term competitive advantage. Every three years it must be thrown out. Our true long-term competitive advantage is our culture and relationships — the people-side of the equation. Providing quality people and support for our agents is one of the hardest things to do, which is why so many new real estate models take the stripped-down approach, it is easier to do and scale. But the hardest things to do are also the hardest to copy and are the most sustainable competitive advantage.

We are staying nimble. If a facilitator role ends up dominating and consumers demonstrate they want that, we will migrate to it. We will have no choice. What we know now is that the best agents are not going to these models. If they do, we will adjust as we always have over the past 90 years.

- **What do you see as the biggest long-term threat to your business?**
The evolution of which service model will best fit the future market. Things are in flux and there is an opportunity to lead the way. The question is can we change deeply and fully enough? As Clayton Christensen laid out in his classic book, *The Innovators Dilemma*, we are working not to get stuck in the incumbency world.

We fear not adjusting enough, making minor tweaks and thinking they are enough, but then getting caught in an unviable model, if the value the market demands shifts to something we are not set up to offer. We must be careful not to get caught in a slow boil. However, we have thrived through industry changes before and we are confident we will this time.

Dan, along with his brother Stuart, serves as co-president of Real Estate One, the largest real estate brokerage in Michigan. Real Estate One has 68 offices and 2,350 agents across Michigan and does $5.6 billion in annual sales. His grandfather, Staunton Elsea, founded Real Estate One in Detroit in 1929. The brothers took the helm in the late 1990s. In addition to the brokerage, Real Estate One operates affiliated businesses including mortgage, title, property insurance and relocation. The company operates under a variety of local brands including Real Estate One, Max Broock Realtors, Reinhart Realtors, Advantage Realty and Johnstone & Johnstone.

08 Blockchain + Real Estate

Redesigning the Brokerage Relationships with Agents and Consumers

Blockchain has generated significant buzz thanks to its novelty, its compelling cryptocurrency application and, in part, its enigmatic, democratic design. Blockchain descriptions get technical and obscure quickly, but real estate leaders need to pay attention as it is poised to play a big role in real estate. While the full scope of blockchain's industry impact will not emerge for some time, useful and compelling applications have already emerged that leverage the technology's strength of efficiently, accurately and securely recording digital events.

This chapter gives real estate brokers an all-purpose guide to real estate and blockchain.

Explaining Blockchain

> "No one really understands blockchain and its potential but it is on track to be probably the industry's next multi-million dollar opportunity."
>
> Stefan Swanepoel

To fully understand how blockchain technology will affect the residential real estate brokerage industry first requires a solid understanding of its basics.

Defining Blockchain

Many brokers and agents have likely heard the term *distributed ledger* to describe blockchain. The term describes the technology well as it reflects the fact that blockchains record events in a chain (or ledger) distributed across a network of computers.

To visualize a blockchain, picture a long chain of individual blocks of information. When a blockchain system records a new event, it cryptographically seals the associated information of who, what and when – called a hash – in a block on a growing chain. Each hash contains unique information of the hash immediately preceding it.

A single block in a blockchain can contain multiple events. A system can use either time (such as 50 milliseconds) or event count (such as a maximum of three events) to determine the size of each block. Once a block meets the predetermined size, the system closes the block. This sealing process involves a reference to the preceding block, which creates a chain – thus the term blockchain.

Each computer in a blockchain network records each new event and verifies its record matches those of all the other networked computers in a practice called reaching consensus. These recordings occur instantaneously in a distributed fashion and require no complex infrastructure or central verification body. Instead, computers in a blockchain network interact as equal players, documenting and verifying events through a peer-to-peer network.

A good blockchain needs enough networked computers to validate the hashes of new blocks in a timely fashion. Computers that validate hashes in a blockchain system are called miners.

The inherent cryptography and redundancy in blockchain technology ensure that information is secure. Changes can only occur by recording a new event subsequent to the original event; the original event remains visible. In this way, blockchains create immutable records.

Deconstructing Blockchain

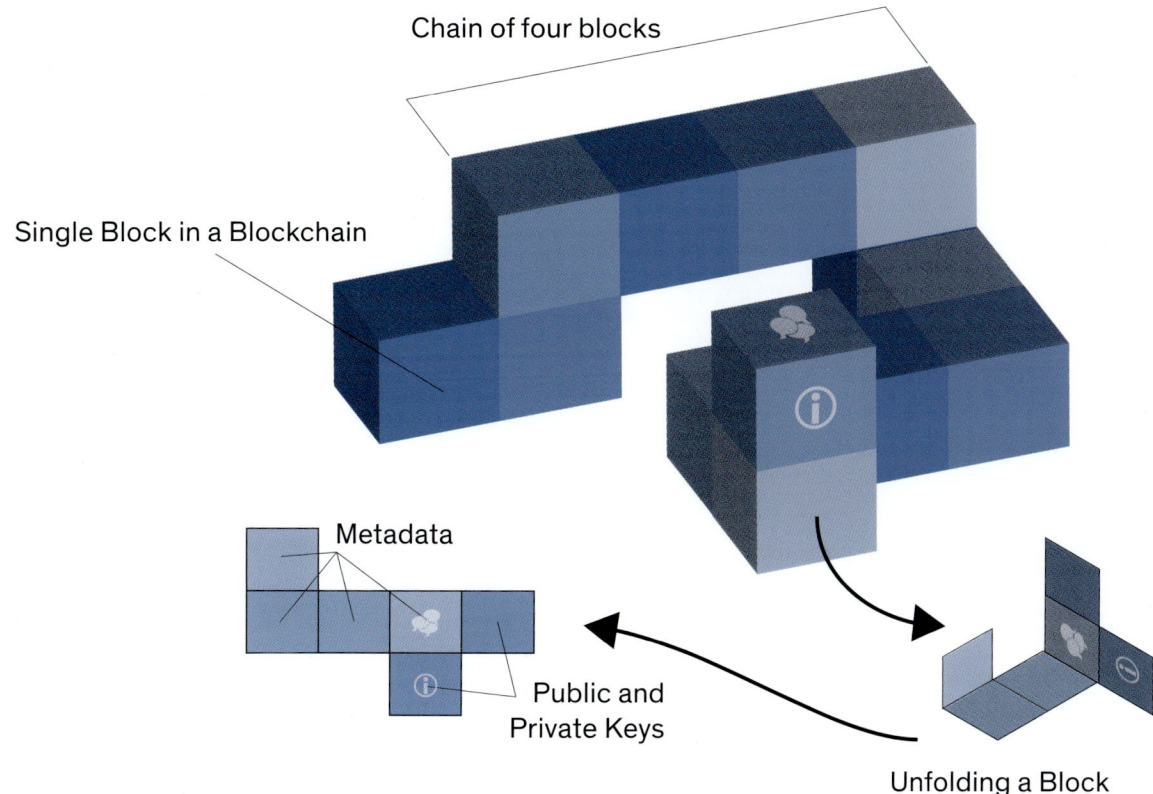

A blockchain is made up of a chain of individual blocks of information, also known as metadata. When a blockchain system records a new event, it cryptographically seals the associated information of who, what and when – called a hash – in a block on a growing chain. Each hash contains unique information of the hash immediately preceding it.

Source: T3 Sixty

Types of Blockchains

Two primary types of blockchains exist: public and private. The difference between the two centers on access and the ability to control access. Generally speaking, everyone can access the information in public blockchains, such as bitcoin and Ethereum. These blockchains are commonly used as a marketplace for commerce, so their transparency is a vital part of their utility.

Private blockchains (also called permissioned blockchains) restrict access to members. They are not public and only members may participate in them. These blockchains are typically designed for asset management; the Realtor Association Blockchain is one such example (See sidebar on page 50).

Realtor Association Blockchain

NAR built the Realtor Association Blockchain to establish a record tied to each member that Realtor associations across the country can access. This helps associations because no central database houses all information relating to members — such as membership status, locations, education and elections. Instead, the industry has over 1,200 distinct Realtor associations divided into national, state and local chapters, each with their own member database. This makes sharing member information difficult — NAR built the Realtor Association Blockchain to solve this.

NAR, along with five state Realtor associations, collaborated on building the Realtor Association Blockchain, which debuted in spring 2018. As a private blockchain, only six operators have a copy of the blockchain, but any association can access it to verify or share member records. The data is encrypted on the blockchain.

With the blockchain, associations can check member status in seconds, a task that previously took emails, phone calls and hours of coordination. In addition, it supports the independence of each Realtor association. Every association is and remains its own business while the Realtor Association Blockchain helps them align around member records in a secure, efficient way.

Blockchain versus Databases

Blockchains are best used for storing permanent data and do not work well for information that requires regular updating or changing.

A helpful analogy is the difference between a driver's license and a driver's record. Information on a person's driver's license changes relatively frequently over time, such as address, appearance (photo) and weight, so it makes sense to store this kind of information in a database that updates periodically. On the other hand, a person's driving record stores an ongoing series of events not subject to change, which makes it a good candidate for blockchain.

The distributed nature of blockchains makes the technology a poor candidate for document storage as a system can have thousands of copies of blockchains, and ensuring that all computers have successfully recorded all the information and verified consistency requires a lot of time and significantly slows down the process. This feature of blockchains makes the technology inferior to databases for storing and frequently changing information.

New ways to improve blockchain storage capability are in development, but not working at full capacity yet.

Blockchain 2.0 and Smart Contracts

The ability to add small conditional programs to blockchains falls into what is sometimes referred to as Blockchain 2.0. Blockchain 2.0 systems incorporate software that enables users to specify rules to a blockchain, such as, "do not execute during business hours," or more complex rules, such as, "on the fourth day, transfer $1,000 to this system."

This type of logic-based blockchain incorporates *smart contracts*, which can be a misleading term because smart contracts differ greatly from legal contracts. A traditional legal contract typically incorporates the outcome of negotiations and often contains various attachments, addenda and amendments tied to a specific transaction. Smart contracts do not describe specific transactions, rather they include the conditional logic upon which an event will occur.

If all the conditions stipulated in a smart contract occur, then the specified event happens. That event could be a disbursement of funds once all conditions of a sale are met, as defined in the smart contract algorithm. A vending machine transaction provides a good example: If someone places the correct amount of the right currency in a vending

> "The distributed nature of blockchains makes the technology a poor candidate for document storage."

> "Smart contracts do not describe specific transactions, rather they include the conditional logic upon which an event will occur."

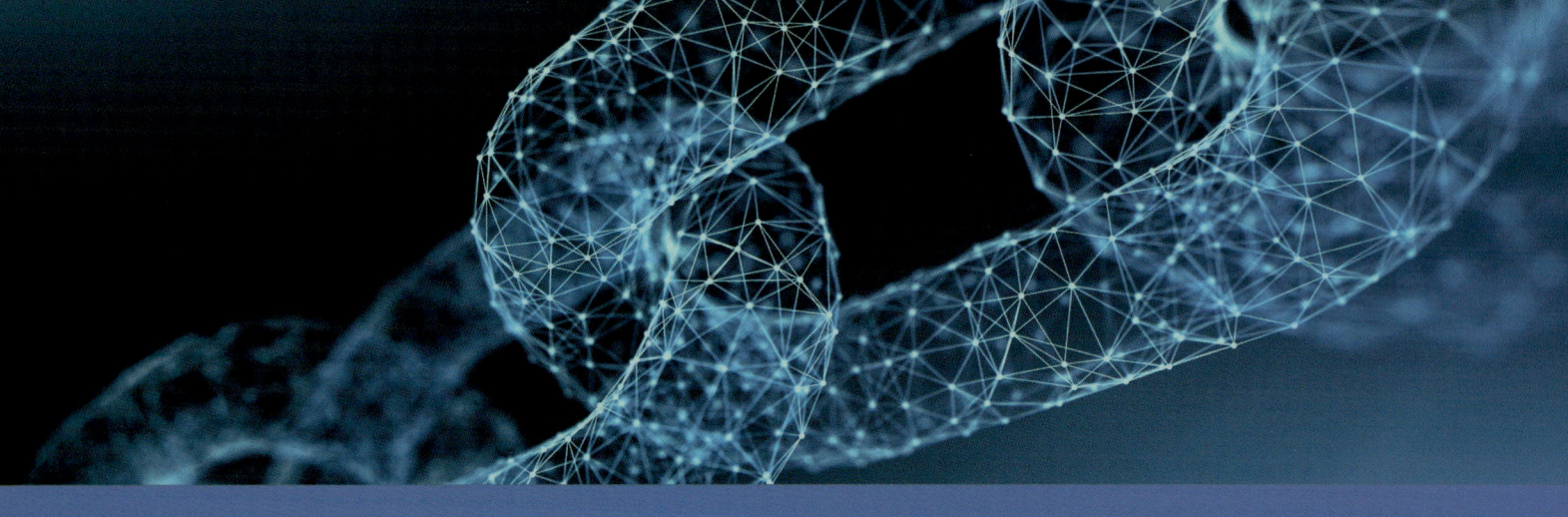

Fraudulent ICOs

ICOs appeal to entrepreneurs because they can use them to raise millions of dollars in a few days with little more than a whitepaper outlining an idea and an attractive website. Over the last several years, some companies have sold shares in an ICO but did not build any products making the tokens worthless and leaving investors with no recourse. The potential for fraud with ICOs is high. In fact, a Bloomberg study revealed that nearly 80 percent of companies valued over $50 million who completed an ICO in 2017 were scams.

machine and selects an in-stock item, the vending machine releases the item (i.e., the smart contract is executed). If those conditions are not met, the item, if present, does not release.

This automatic execution feature of smart contracts and Blockchain 2.0 can lead to unintended consequences as it can be difficult to control; a smart contract may not be robust enough to capture all possible reasons not to execute an event, for example. Blockchains such as Ethereum govern transactions with smart contracts. Other systems have the same capability but use different terminology for this feature. Hyperledger, for example, uses the term Chaincode.

Blockchains with smart contracts are potentially disruptive as they could facilitate financial transactions without middlemen such as banks.

Cryptocurrency

Bitcoin first gained a wide following in 2009, a year after the pseudonymous creator Satoshi Nakamoto detailed the cryptocurrency in a paper titled, "Bitcoin: A peer-to-Peer Electronic Cash System." Bitcoin, of course, became the first well-known cryptocurrency.

Cryptocurrencies are a well-publicized application of blockchain. Blockchain technology include tradeable value because the computers

> "Although cryptocurrencies can be traded as an equity or commodity, they do not correlate with any current financial instruments."

in a blockchain network must record, verify and store the data associated with blockchain events. The system compensates the owners of those computers for that work in cryptocurrency.

Computers powering a blockchain are said to be mining. In many cases, the owners of these computers are compensated for this with cryptocurrency tokens or coins (coins and tokens have the same meaning with respect to blockchain and cryptocurrency). Owners of these tokens can then trade them on a cryptocurrency exchange, allowing others to invest in them. Some blockchains, called permissioned blockchains (such as Hyperledger), do not require cryptocurrency to operate.

Typically, companies looking to build blockchain-based products will offer tokens for sale to investors to raise capital before building a product. These offers, known as initial coin offerings (ICO), have the same purpose as initial public offerings (IPO) – to raise cash from investors by offering shares of a company. Unlike IPOs, the US Securities and Exchange Commission does not regulate ICOs. The ICO approach typically involves offshore banking and legal mechanisms designed to avoid SEC regulation. However, the SEC has published guidelines for investors to consider when deciding on whether to invest in a company through an ICO (sec.gov/ICO).

Some companies use ICOs in place of traditional seed and angel investment to bypass the normal venture capital fundraising process. Most companies ICO fall under that bucket, but this avenue's popularity is waning.

Cryptocurrency as Investment

Cryptocurrencies have received significant media coverage in recent years. Many, no doubt, have heard of the major blockchain-based cryptocurrencies bitcoin and Ethereum and their volatile history — both have experienced spectacular 10X value surges as well as meteoric meltdowns.

These cryptocurrencies trade much like traditional commodities such as wheat, corn and oil. Due to the investment medium's newness and the uncertainty investors have about it, cryptocurrency values have been volatile, experiencing dramatic shifts. Indeed, the sensationalism tied to these swings tend to drown out other dynamic blockchain applications.

Although cryptocurrencies can be traded as an equity or commodity, they do not correlate with any current financial instruments. The market swings exist because these cryptocurrencies experience much more pronounced network effects. For example, Google searches, social media and forum posts correlate highly with increases in bitcoin price.

> "Cryptocurrency tokens come in two types: security tokens and utility tokens."

Cryptocurrency tokens come in two types: security tokens and utility tokens. Both kinds of tokens have value and can be traded. Security tokens give owners a share in the company offering them. Utility tokens, on the other hand, carry no company ownership but give owners access to a good or service, much as a person can use laundry tokens to activate a washing machine.

While these two cryptocurrency types exist, no entity regulates them, so the parameters around them remain murky.

Investing in blockchains as a cryptocurrency and using the technology for other applications is an important difference. The monetary value some blockchains carry represent just one aspect of their utility, and not the most interesting or useful for real estate. When applied as a tool, they are a unique and useful way to record and verify events.

Blockchain Strengths and Weaknesses

Blockchain Strengths

- Blockchains do not require backups because multiple full copies exist on distinct computers; this built-in redundancy ensures that damaged, altered or lost copies do not affect the recording of a blockchain event. The multiple copies ensure that the correct record remains.

- Uptime improves because as long as a computer has internet access, event information remains available.

- Depending on the application and user base size, operating a blockchain can be inexpensive because blockchains require no special software and no backup mechanisms. (For public blockchains, however, participants need sufficient hard drive or server space to retain a full copy of the entire blockchain they use.)

- A blockchain network keeps a permanent, cryptographically sealed copy of each record, making information on a blockchain extremely secure. Once recorded, an event is tamperproof.

- Identifying fraud is straightforward with blockchain as each record contains a timestamp. Computers in a blockchain network can stop trusting a computer with an irregular record.

Blockchain Weaknesses

- As networked computers must copy entire blockchains upon recording an event, the system can bog down as blockchains get longer and longer. Bitcoin and Ethereum, for example, have become geometrically slower over time as they grow larger. As recently as two years ago, bitcoin transactions took just a few minutes. Now, because of bitcoin's bulky size, transactions take between thirty minutes to as long a day. However, developers are coming up with workarounds. Experts believe that speeds will drastically increase in the coming years.

- Blockchains require huge storage capacity as each recorded event requires each networked computer to make and store a full copy of the full chain.

- Blockchain technology can fail when users misapply it such as using it when a database would better serve or rushing to an ICO with no product delivery plan.

> "Blockchain has generated significant buzz thanks to its novelty, its compelling cryptocurrency application and, in part, its enigmatic, democratic design."

Real Estate Blockchain Applications

There are several real estate industry blockchain applications currently in use, including those that verify identities and credentials of parties in a transaction and enable fractional real estate ownership. These and other promising real estate blockchain applications are outlined below.

Security and Verification

Blockchains can identify, verify and store identities, which are an important, time-consuming, complicated and expensive part of the current real estate process.

The Realtor Association Blockchain does this. NAR has placed its membership roster on a private blockchain accessible to any Realtor association nationwide. Those wanting to access the blockchain,

Future Blockchain Timeline

Blockchain technology is in its infancy, so making accurate predictions of its potential real estate impact is speculative, but T3 Sixty decided to create a timeline of potential real estate blockchain developments. These are not predictions, but simply speculations to provide readers a window into where blockchain could head. Events in the periods below will overlap and may change as the industry shifts and new legislation appears.

2019 - 2021	Indexing, asset-management and fractional ownership will become major real estate blockchain applications. In this application, other systems verify user identity and credential using blockchain-based tools.
2021 - 2023	Blockchain-based services will take root in real estate, most likely in the form of tasks agents must frequently do, such as preparing transaction documents. They will include smart contract functionality, which will help automate some tasks. Tokens will become a promising payment for these services, as an alternative to credit cards and fund transfers, which could eliminate or significantly reduce mortgage fraud.
2023 - 2025	By this time, enough blockchain technology will have been tested that the industry will know where it is most effective — the winning blockchain real estate applications will emerge.
2025 - 2027	Real estate blockchain applications will integrate deeply with each other, which will uncover benefits not yet clear today.
2027 - 2029	With blockchain applications clearly defined, accepted and widely used, government and regulatory agencies will step in and attempt to regulate them.

Source: T3 Sixty

contact the operators and, if approved, receive credentials to access the data. When Realtors move across country, for example, their Realtor information and credentials travel with them, verifiable on the association blockchain. Previously, local associations had no easy way to verify or access this information.

Fractional Ownership

Real estate investment trusts (REITs) own or finance income-producing real estate through investor pools. This fractional property ownership is an ideal application for blockchain and is already in use in some countries. To establish fractional ownership, these tools distribute tokens. Each token represents a share of real property, not a value of an exchange-traded cryptocurrency such as bitcoin and Ethereum.

Consumers use tokens to both pay for stakes and receive income from rent or a sale. Owners and operators can further subdivide fractional shares and sell them without the permission of any controlling entity. The system requires no minimum investment because the market requires little overhead; operators collect cash in exchange for issuing tokens. In addition, no minimum ownership timeframes exist and participants may sell their shares to anyone the minute they care to.

Unlike REITs, blockchain-powered fractional ownership has no regulation requirements. In some countries, such as South Korea, the government ensures that fractional owners receive payment when a property sells by issuing a lien in the name of the operator.

Blockchain-based fractional ownership companies are popping up around the world. Below are a few that have launched in the last twenty-four months:

- PropertyShare.in (India, propertyshare.in)
- Meridio (formerly Pangea, US, meridio.co)
- ChromaWay (Sweden, chromaway.com)
- REIDAO (Singapore, reidao.io)
- BlochExchange (Australia, blochexchange.com)
- Proof Suite (Korea, proofsuite.com)
- Blocksquare (Slovenia, blocksquare.io)

Purchasing Property with Cryptocurrency

Cryptocurrency sales in the US predominantly involve buyers cashing out of their cryptocurrency on an exchange and then paying for the property in cash.

Although the number of cryptocurrency transactions will likely increase over time, they will remain a very small percentage of the market until big banks get involved with cryptocurrency, because so many home purchases involve bank financing. This will not likely happen any time soon as FDIC-insured banks — virtually all banks in the US — avoid trading in extremely volatile commodities such as cryptocurrency.

Also, brokers, agents and sellers will not likely list properties in cryptocurrency in the foreseeable future, other than to generate buzz. Although buyers can use cryptocurrency to pay for items, nailing a home's list price — or sale price for that matter — can prove difficult if not impossible because cryptocurrency value changes frequently, often on an hourly basis.

Buyers and sellers complete home transactions overwhelmingly with government-backed currency, and will continue to do so for the foreseeable future.

Streamlining the Transaction Process

Some companies use blockchain technology to improve the transaction process. Two of these include ShelterZoom (shelterzoom.com) and Imbrex (formerly RexMLS, imbrex.io). Both firms have significant financial backing and use tokens to execute the transaction process rather than for properties themselves.

Launched in 2017, ShelterZoom allows homebuyers and renters to make offers on a property using Ethereum blockchain-based technology. The system uses smart contracts to execute a deal; once all conditions are met and parties agree, a deal goes through. Users pay an $8 fee for the service.

Imbrex, which launched in 2018, is attempting to build an international blockchain-based listing database. On the Imbrex platform, buyers and sellers can negotiate price, make and accept offers and other actions around the transaction. They pay for these services with coins they buy from Imbrex. When it comes time to execute a transaction, they pay with traditional currency.

Blockchain Data Standards

A handful of groups in the residential real estate brokerage space have already begun working to create industry standards for blockchains: the Real Estate Standards Organization (RESO, reso.org) and the Mortgage Industry Standards Maintenance Organization (MISMO, mismo.org).

In 2018, RESO established the Distributed Ledger Workgroup to address blockchain technology. The workgroup is working to define and

> "Agents could use a blockchain-based tool to optimize their lead-conversion process."

document the events related to a property such as improvements, taxes and the listing and closing process to prepare them for blockchain use. The workgroup also maintains and frequently updates a blockchain terms and jargon document.

In 2017, MISMO created a Blockchain Community of Practice workgroup to discuss early blockchain technology pilots, use-cases and jargon. Although only at the discussion phase, the MISMO group has a goal of publishing blockchain best practices, creating prototypes and providing education to its membership.

A third group, International Blockchain in Real Estate Association (IBREA, ibrea.network), focuses on blockchain education and sharing information in the real estate industry. Instead of setting standards, the nonprofit group uses a chapter model to foster industry blockchain education.

"The inherent cryptography and redundancy in blockchain technology ensure that information is secure."

Potential Real Estate Blockchain Applications

Optimizing Client Acquisition

Some companies, including those in real estate, are beginning to leverage blockchain technology to record the steps that lead to a client acquisition.

For example, a blockchain can be used to record when clients open an email, when they visit a website, how quickly they respond to a text message and more.

"Blockchains are great for this because they are optimized for recording events in time."

These records can be immensely valuable in training artificial intelligence systems to predict which contacts are most likely to become clients and prescribe steps – or even automate them – to turn them into clients. Blockchains are great for this because they are optimized for recording events in time – they do it well and efficiently.

This same blockchain application could be applied to other real estate scenarios, such as listing and marketing a home. Agents could use a blockchain tool to record the steps they took to sell a home, along with all the circumstances surrounding it — market heat, price, specific location, condition, relative value and more — and feed this into an artificially intelligent system that optimizes their home selling strategy.

Seamless Property Transfers

Many hope that technology will facilitate seamless property transfers. Some expect that blockchains, embedded with smart contracts, will make this dream a reality. In this scenario, a transaction would proceed automatically as conditions baked into a smart contract-powered blockchain are met.

The single-platform, automated transaction goal remains extremely idealistic as the players who must collaborate come from different industries, each with its own set of rules and business practices. Some of these practices exist by convention, others by consensus and others by legislative or regulatory action. Many of the players are well-established companies, with little incentive to change. (See current industry efforts to create an all-encompassing real estate transaction platform in "The Digital Closing," Trend No. 7.)

The data within each industry lives in databases that require upstream and downstream data translation by participants in distinct industries including title, mortgage, brokerage, credit, legal, inspection, appraising, insurance, and county records, to name just a few. Currently, just two of these industries have begun work toward data standardization. The hurdles of standardizing in just one industry are immense, so the idea that multiple industries will standardize their data for efficient use in other industries remains an extremely high bar.

Multiple industries developing interoperability rarely occurs without government intervention. If a single association that addressed the entire real estate transaction existed — a National Real Estate

> "Blockchain technology will not likely change the way buyers pay for property."

Transaction Processors Association, for example – it could create standards that apply across the entire transaction. Time will tell if this happens; if it does, it is many years away.

Takeaway

Despite the widespread cryptocurrency buzz, blockchain technology will not likely change the way buyers pay for property. Instead, it will increasingly streamline processes around the transaction such as repetitive tasks real estate agents do, the verification of user identities and credentials and drive additional real estate fractional ownership applications.

Blockchain already powers tools with these applications today. In the future, blockchain will likely also optimize brokers' and agents' client acquisition strategies with its ability to easily and quickly record events. The data integrity and cost-savings that blockchain applications bring to real estate are clear. If this technology also speeds up transactions, adoption will accelerate.

Blockchain technology and applications are rapidly evolving. Over the next few years, industry leaders will need to monitor its progress closely to fully understand and leverage its full utility and mitigate its risks, many of which remain unclear. T3 Sixty will continue to analyze this trend as it develops.

Lead Contributors:

Mark Lesswing
Mark served as the Chief Technology Officer of the National Association of Realtors from 2006 to 2018. He currently serves as Blockchain Technology Officer at DomiDocs Inc. Mark is a frequent speaker at major trade conferences and is very active in the open source software community. The views expressed in this article are those of the Mark and T3 Sixty and do not necessarily reflect the views of Mark's former employer, NAR. Mark can be reached at mark@lesswing.com.

Paul Hagey
Paul is Executive Editor of the Swanepoel Trends Report, founding Publisher of Boulder, Colorado, magazine BLDRfly and runs the content agency HageyMedia. He began covering the real estate industry as fulltime reporter with Inman News, where he became an award-winning journalist. Paul is a graduate of the University of Missouri Graduate School of Journalism. Paul can be reached at paul@t360.com.

07 The Digital End-To-End Real Estate Transaction Dream

Closer than Ever, But Still Far Away.

The standard residential real estate transaction involves hundreds of detailed financial requirements, legal contracts and many other real estate forms involving dozens of documents and multiple parties. Transaction participants include appraisers, title examiners, home inspectors, pest inspection personnel, surveyors, engineers, buyers, sellers, buyer's and seller's agents, loan officers, underwriters, attorneys for buyers and sellers, closing staff and more.

Most of these participants work in industries with their own particular procedures and requirements, which makes integrating all the transaction steps together in a seamless process difficult. This chapter presents an overview of a few of the industries critical to the residential real estate transaction process and the steps some have taken to develop an all-digital closing

> "The most powerful real estate dream of the last twenty-five years still has not reached reality. Long live one-stop shopping."
>
> Stefan Swanepoel

The Disjointed Transaction

The vast majority of real estate consumers view the homebuying transaction process with anxiety and frustration. The annual trillion dollar industry has not created a smooth, seamless, digital process for consumers or the various professional parties involved. While some individual transactions steps have become digitized, the transaction process, as a whole, remains one mired in paperwork, mismatched standards and highly localized.

Given the broad scope and multiplicity of players with their respective digital systems, consumers find it difficult to keep track of all the steps of a closing. In addition, the communication between parties that push a transaction to a close runs the full medium gamut—snail mail, phone call, email, fax, hand deliveries and text message—muddying the process even further. When confronted by the mass of old-school paperwork and disconnected procedures of the current transaction process, consumers rightly express frustration and confusion.

The pain point here for consumers is real. Anyone who has bought or sold a property recognizes the long, often complicated and disjointed process, often laden with paper. Just as they have done with many other industries, outside investors are now pouring funding into the problem to find the holy grail of a consumer-centric digital real estate transaction experience. Consumers are used to a smooth digital experience in almost every other area of their lives such as banking, travel, hospitality, medicine and retail. The real estate closing process is overdue for a digital makeover.

The Vision

The vision for a digital contact-to-contract-to-close real estate platform has been in the industry since the early eighties when Sears attempted to bring a full-service transaction to life by owning Dean Witter Financial Services, Allstate Insurance and Coldwell Banker. After many false starts and failed promises, technology now exists that enables that end-to-end platform. Industry participants understand the need for standardization and the deep allure of the end-to-end digital process, and with funding, at least for now at an almost endless supply, this vision is back on the table.

Industries are beginning to take steps. For example, consider the current homebuying process. It typically starts with buyers searching for a home online on a site such as Zillow or realtor.com. But this breaks down when a mortgage enters the equation. Buyers who need financing—and most of them do—really can afford only a subset of those homes. Some mortgage companies are looking to preapprove buyers and show them only homes they can afford based on their preapproval. When buyers choose a home on that platform, their financial information seamlessly follows them to the financing part of the process. This is just one example of how industries are streamlining the digital transaction.

The Transaction Unscrambled

While identifying and describing the procedural steps of a typical real estate transaction and especially the financing and legal closing process is relatively easy, the process remains one of the most perplexing and intimidating experiences consumers will face in their life. For context of what steps an end-to-end digital platform—or more likely, an integrated set of platforms—would need to incorporate, the steps of a real estate transaction are presented below:

Step 1 - Purchase Agreement Signed

A purchase, or buy-sell, agreement between a buyer and seller typically kicks off the traditional transaction. The listing brokerage is normally responsible for selecting the closing agency (escrow or attorney) if the buy-sell agreement does not specify one. Participants: Buyers, sellers, listing agent and buyer's agent (if used).

Step 2 - Open Escrow

Upon receiving the executed buy-sell agreement, the closing agency opens an escrow account. This is commonly referred to as opening escrow. The escrow account is a highly regulated special third-party account that holds funds on behalf of the buyer and seller and enables a smooth transaction between the parties. Participants: Buyers, sellers and the closing agency.

Step 3 - Do a Title Search, Obtain Title Insurance

The next step involves ordering a title search and a title insurance policy. These documents ensure sellers, in fact, own the property they are trying to sell and uncover any previously conveyed rights associated with the property such as mortgages, easements leases or other rights of possession and ownership.

Real Estate Transactional Steps Unscrambled

While identifying and describing the procedural steps of a typical real estate transaction and especially the financing and legal closing process is relatively easy, the process remains one of the most perplexing and intimidating experiences consumers will face in their entire life.

Here is a high-level view of the steps in the current process:

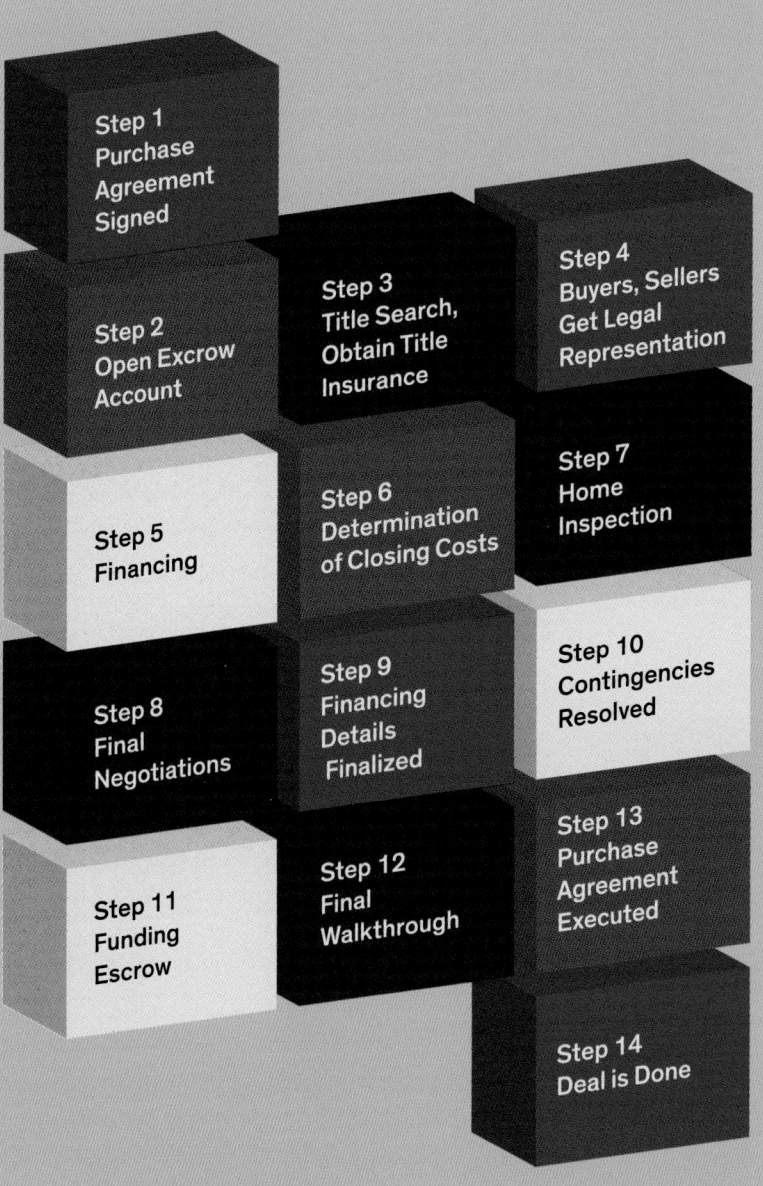

Source: T3 Sixty

In some states, especially those that do not require title policies, a title officer will perform a title search to ensure there are no encumbrances to a clear title. Where title insurance will be used, the title insurance agency performs a title search. Participants: Title insurance agency.

Step 4 - Buyers, Sellers Get Legal Representation

The next step involves the buyer and seller securing legal representation where necessary. Some states require legal representation, others do not. A significant amount of research and experience has established that few consumers, even the most sophisticated ones, really understand the impact and ramifications of what may well be up to fifty pages of legal jargon in closing documents. Participants: Lawyers.

Step 5 - Financing

The majority of purchase transactions involve buyer financing. While this is not actually part of the legal closing process, it is often a huge component. Participants: Buyers and the mortgage company.

Step 6 - Determination of Closing Costs

At this step, some transactions involve the determination of closing costs and which parties will pay them.

To qualify as closing costs, these expenses and fees must be paid to the closing agency. This differentiates closing costs from other non-closing fees and expenses connected to third-party services such as real estate brokerage commissions and mortgage-related fees. This step is sometimes omitted. Participants: Buyers, sellers, listing agent (if used) and buyer's agent (if used).

Step 7 - Home Inspection

Home inspections are not normally required by law and therefore are not formally part of the closing process, but most purchase agreements and lenders require it.

In most situations, valid or qualifying defects discovered during the inspection either require resolution by the seller or can be grounds for terminating the purchase agreement. Pest inspections, too, are not mandatory in most states but most purchase agreements and mortgage lenders require them. Participants: Inspectors, buyers, seller and the mortgage company.

Step 8 - Final Negotiations

Typically, at some point prior to the formal and final closing process, buyers and sellers will meet to discuss and renegotiate the financial details of the transaction in light of any defects, damages or new conditions discovered during the escrow period. Participants: Buyers, sellers, listing agent (if used), buyer's agent (if used).

Step 9 - Financing Details Finalized

As the formal closing date approaches, buyers will complete final negotiations with their mortgage lender and lock in their mortgage rate. This is not part of the actual closing process, but it is a critical detail that can bring the closing to a halt if not resolved. Participants: Buyers and the mortgage company.

Step 10 - Contingencies Resolved

As a closing nears completion, parties will resolve each of the contingencies reflected in the purchase agreement. These usually involve financing, major defects and problems relating to the physical property and legal status requirements.

Contingencies must be resolved in writing on or before a closing becomes official. Participants: Buyers, sellers, the mortgage company and the closing agency.

Step 11 - Funding Escrow

Another critical step before a transaction is finalized is funding escrow. The basis of the transaction is conveying clear title to the property in return for providing the full purchase amount specified.

This usually involves deposits, down payments and mortgage proceeds. The money used to fund the transaction must be provided to escrow and must be free and clear in the transaction escrow account. Participants: Buyers, the mortgage company and the escrow agency.

Step 12 - Final Walkthrough

While not generally required by law, purchase agreements typically call for a final walkthrough before final closing. The walkthrough gives the buyer a final opportunity to determine that no damage or other changes have occurred to the property since the purchase was negotiated and executed. Participants: Buyers, sellers, listing agent (if used), buyer's agent (if used).

Step 13 - Purchase Agreement Executed

A contract is executed as outlined in the purchase agreement with all the documents necessary to convey property title and resolve any remaining contingencies and complete requirements connected to the funding process. Participants: Buyers, listing agent and buyer's agent.

Step 14 - Deal Is Done

The deal is now done. Sellers receive the agreed upon payment and buyers receive title to the property. Occupancy of the property usually occurs on the same date, although it can be earlier or later if determined by the contract and compensated accordingly. Participants: Buyers, sellers and the escrow agency.

End-to-End Transactional Dream

Challenges

The primary industries involved in a real estate transaction include brokerage, mortgage, title insurance and escrow or settlement services. Homeowners insurance and home warranty supplement a transaction but are not core as the above four industries are. The nonprofit Real Estate Service Providers Council (RESPRO, respro.org) is working to unify these industries.

The technology exists to make a fully digital end-to-end digital experience possible. The laws exist to make it possible. But the multiple-industry, fragmented market hampers the vision, as does the fact that cross-industry standards and the ability to integrate disparate platforms remain a big dream.

Data Standards

Exacerbating the integration of these industries is the lack of standards and the inability of smaller software vendors to offer smooth integration with other platforms.

Brokerage is furthest along thanks to the Real Estate Standards Organization (RESO, reso.org), which is developing nationwide standards for the way the industry defines and moves data through the Data Dictionary and Web API. See Trend No. 5 for more.

The mortgage industry has developed standards for its industry through the Mortgage Industry Standards Maintenance Organization (mismo.org). RESO and MISMO are just beginning to collaborate on cross-industry standards, but this is very early in what promises to be a long process.

Title insurance, which covers the act of verifying whether a person selling a property actual owns the title free and clear, and escrow, which ensures all the money and docs go to the correct places in a closing, are much further out from developing standards. This is in large part because, unlike brokerage and mortgage, which typically have practices that vary state by state, their operations often vary by county. With more than 3,000 recording jurisdictions in the US, nationwide standardization is many years, if not decades, away.

Lack of Integration

Even if data standards were fully complete across real estate, mortgage, title and settlement, each industry has its own variety of platforms and they do not seamlessly integrate. As the recent influx of venture capital has spawned a new round of transaction management, loan origination and title production systems, the result is a many-to-many relationship, where no single platform currently, or in the near future, has all of the necessary integrations.

Whose Closing Platform

As mentioned above, currently, there are dozens of systems that aim to bring all parties together for a digital transaction. Each industry—brokerage, mortgage, title and escrow—has its own proprietary system and procedures, making cross-industry collaboration difficult.

There is no industry-neutral platform that all participants currently choose to use. Each industry has its own workflow and process. If a transaction starts in a digital transaction management platform such as DocuSign, SkySlope or dotloop, for example, all parties could theoretically meet there and complete a transaction, but this does not happen because each industry wants to own its piece of the transaction, often because they are more familiar with it and feel they can reduce risk.

Currently, when a transaction progresses through the brokerage phase and is ready for the mortgage and other phases, it is usually easier for participants to just email a PDF of the necessary docs rather than negotiate whose platform to use and how. The same goes for the other settlement service providers.

Fraud Risk

The risk of cyber fraud is high in real estate. Cyber thieves have set up a wide variety of elaborate schemes. Wire fraud is a growing issue that has cost many consumers huge amounts of their personal savings with fraudulent emails remaining a large factor here.

> "The risk of cyber fraud is high in real estate."

So, new processes and technology unfamiliar and untested by real estate pros in different segments of the transaction can be viewed as unpopular and just not worth the risk. Also, smaller companies have difficulty in keeping up with the advancements and spend required to guarantee security. Given that title and escrow typically vary by county, a paper document sometimes becomes the easiest, simplest, most consistent way for firms to guarantee closings occur in a compliant, risk-mitigated manner.

Movement Toward a Digital Transaction

Some of the necessary steps for a full, seamless digital transaction are taking place. For example, more states are allowing remote digital closings—where buyers and sellers do not have to show up in person to sign closing documents. Instead, they can do a Remote Online Notarization (RON). These closings take place with sophisticated new RON technology that verifies buyer and borrower driver's licenses, facilitates e-signatures and captures both the remote notary and buyers on video.

This requires that each lender, borrower and title company on a transaction have the processes in place to support a remote notary. In addition, the transaction also must fall within a county that records real estate documents electronically, also known as e-recording. Given these complexities, it is often easier just to print and sign, though consumers are increasingly demanding more convenient options for real estate closings.

While RON closings are becoming more popular, they face many of the same hurdles that in-person electronic closings, otherwise known as eClosings, face. Electronic closings have long been available, but have not been widely adopted because mortgage lenders often do not know which investor will ultimately purchase a loan at origination—some require wet signatures.

Digitizing the Transaction

Although all the parties know what to do, and real estate agents and escrow companies coordinate the process start to finish, there is no predominant technology platform that enables everyone to participate in one overarching system.

In recent years, several firms have started to develop overarching systems that can function as an end-to-end platform. These companies are attempting to build a platform that will bring together brokerage firms, mortgage companies, title companies, homeowner insurance firms, inspectors and closing companies.

While the specifics of design and function of each of these parties may vary slightly, the vision and basic steps will conform to the closing steps outlined above. To be efficient, the platform must also be transparent to consumers. The process must cover all administrative, legal, regulatory and informational needs for all transaction participants.

The end-to-end digital closing will likely require multiple, integrated platforms. Each separate system would transmit the required authenticated information between authorized parties. There is movement to an underlying authorized digital exchange of information between the new generation of systems with highly documented, scalable and secure APIs.

An end-to-end, digital contact-to-contract-to-close experience will include much of the following:

- A closing and settlement process real estate consumers can follow easily and understand. It should be consumer-centric.
- A universal closing performance standard that governs the closing and settlement process. All parties in the closing process must accept and use it.

- Allow consumers choices in closing options ranging from the existing paper model to full digital closing or eClosing. With eClosing models including in-person options and the newer Remote Online Notarization technology, consumers have more options than ever before.

- An end-to-end audit trail.

- Perform digital closings, but also have the flexibility to print documents for wet signatures (if required during the transition to technology) and scan them back in for digital viewing and storage.

The Real Estate Brokerage Digital Marketplace

Real estate brokerages have long understood and seen the value of running multiple profit channels by owning affiliated businesses that support their brokerage role. These include mortgage, insurance and title. So, of course, streamlining the closing process has always made sense.

In addition to large, established brokerages working toward building their own backend, secure, digital end-to-end platforms, newer real estate companies are also making similar efforts.

Both Realogy and HomeServices of America, along with many brokerages, own and operate significant affiliated business subsidiaries. They, of course, cannot mandate their brokerage clients to use their affiliated services but they can, via RESPA-compliant means, advise and encourage them of the benefits of an integrated service. These companies process as much of the real estate transaction as they can digitally but the transaction still breaks down along the way with the inefficiencies and paper that real estate professionals and consumers know all too well.

New players Redfin, Opendoor and Zillow Group all have talked about streamlining the transaction for consumers—Redfin, for example, has a stated goal of reducing its average number of days to close from thirty to seven with an end-to-end platform — but time will tell if it will achieve this. It, of course, is not alone in hunting this Holy Grail.

> "In recent years, several firms have started to develop overarching systems that can function as an end-to-end platform."

The Mortgage Digital Marketplace

Mortgage companies are increasingly focusing on the lifetime value of their customers. They are consistently looking for ways to start their client relationship earlier in the homeownership journey and making large investments to lock in a more seamless loan origination experience.

The ability to verify property and borrower data, as well as a secure, private, compliant method for transferring information to authorized parties makes a digital mortgage possible. A digitized version of the Fannie Mae Uniform Residential Loan Application 1003 — the industry standard form for mortgage applications used for nearly all mortgage loans in the US — is now supported by more than a dozen loan origination systems with direct access to Fannie Mae's online origination system Desktop Originator.

Where once humans reviewed and verified a borrower's employment, income, asset and credit history on paper, products such as AccountChek and AssetReport from FormFree (formfree.com) accomplish these tasks for mortgage lenders in seconds. These products also maintain full compliance and integration with the Fannie Mae Desktop Underwriter system. There are now twenty-six other vendors who have partnered with Fannie Mae to expedite the digital verification of borrower data for underwriting.

The digitization and verification of the mortgage origination process increasingly enables the industry to become more comfortable with moving sensitive borrower and property data digitally.

With years of historic low interest rates, fewer homeowners will refinance their mortgages and be more likely to remain in a servicer's portfolio until they sell their home.

> "Approximately 55 million homeowners make a mortgage payment every month to a loan servicer so this enormous client base remains a very important and large source of revenue and future transaction opportunities."

Approximately 55 million homeowners make a mortgage payment every month to a loan servicer so this enormous client base remains a very important and large source of revenue and future transaction opportunities.

Unbalanced competition will however heat up (as it has in the past) because, while federally chartered banks are prohibited from owning a real estate brokerage, mortgage lenders do not have such restrictions.

So when large mortgage companies start taking steps to build a digital real estate platform that spans beyond mortgage, industry participants take notice. Rock Holdings Inc., parent company of the nation's largest loan originator Quicken Loans (quickenloans.com), has undertaken one such initiative; it is currently spreading its wings to get closer to real estate consumers. In September 2018, it rebranded its real estate agent referral network In-House Realty to Rocket Homes (rockethomes.com) to better align with Quicken Loans' Rocket Mortgage and RocketLoans brands.

The consumer-facing site allows homebuyers to search for homes and also a mortgage, from an integrated platform, which claims to deliver consumers a loan preapproval within eight minutes. The portal, which plans to have national listing coverage by 2019, features a Quicken Loans mortgage preapproval widget prominently on listings. The company wants to help buyers understand what they can afford during their search—when they sign up for a mortgage, they integrate their home search with the mortgage process—they share one login for Rocket Mortgage and Rocket Homes.

Rocket Homes has a nationwide referral network of 25,000 agents. When consumers are ready to work with an agent, Rocket Homes connects them with one of its referral agents and collects a referral fee. In May 2018, In-House Realty (before its Rocket Homes rebrand), acquired FSBO site ForSaleByOwner.com.

This is just one example of a company working to execute on all-digital closing vision.

The Title Insurance Digital Marketplace

Title insurance protects lenders and homebuyers from issues related to faulty titles. It is a major component of home sales in the US.

A major title insurance player, Fidelity National Financial (fnf.com), is making moves to build an end-to-end real estate digital platform that will take consumers from contact through contract to close. Even before the 2018 announcement of Fidelity's potential acquisition of large title insurer Stewart Title, Fidelity's title wing was the nation's largest. The firm spun off major MLS software provider Black Knight (blackknightinc.com) in 2017 but remains connected; Fidelity nonexecutive chairman William P. Foley, II remains executive chairman of Black Knight.

The firm has publicly revealed its intentions to build a real estate platform. It has stated that if consumers want to sell their house they will be able to list it through one of its technology companies and then provide them other products and services such as homeowner's insurance, pest control and home inspection through the platform. The firm is mainly looking to build a compliant, risk-averse transaction platform for real estate professionals that will enhance the consumer experience every step of the way through a transaction.

A slew of acquisitions has underscored this vision. In July 2016, Fidelity acquired real estate lead-gen and CRM platform Commission Inc. (CINC; commissionsinc.com) for $250 million. CINC product offerings include software, marketing and real estate related services for agents and teams. At the time of the acquisition, CINC had more than 1,500 customers who collectively closed over 170,000 residential real estate transactions over the previous twelve months.

Then in July 2017, Fidelity acquired real estate agent CRM and marketing platform Real Geeks (realgeeks.com). The Real Geek acquisition marked another step by Fidelity to broaden its position in the real estate marketplace. Upon the date of purchase Real Geeks had 3,100 clients.

In October 2017, FNF announced that it acquired a majority stake in popular digital transaction management platform SkySlope (skyslope.com) used by many of the nation's largest brokerages. In 2018, SkySlope served 1,700 brokerages representing 160,000 agents.

Known as a shrewd and smart investor, nonexecutive Chairman Bill Foley now has many significant components to build a full-featured real estate platform.

> "The long-held dream of the all-digital, seamless real estate transaction is taking shape, though it is still many years away."

Takeaway

The long-held dream of the all-digital, seamless real estate transaction is taking shape, though it is still many years away.

While electronic closings are becoming more widely accepted in states and counties across the country and by an increasing number of companies, the lack of cross-industry standards and platforms hamper real estate consumers and professionals from enjoying an all-digital, contract-to-close transaction any time soon.

But consumers are coming to expect the simplicity and convenience a digital transaction provides in their real estate experience. Investors are squarely focused on funding products that support this—when consumers get a taste, growth and adoption will accelerate.

At some point, the adjacent real estate industries will have to work together to create cross-industry standards and protocols to support safe, compliant transfers of data in secure ways. This, along with a standardization of local settlement laws and practices, will help make this dream a reality. The all-digital real estate transaction will not happen without these movements.

Real estate brokerage companies, mortgage companies and title companies are all racing separately to build the platform that allows them to better control and own more of the consumer's real estate business than they traditionally have.

When completed, these tools will fundamentally alter the relationship consumers in very fundamental ways. Brokers and agents will face significant competition, both upstream and downstream of the consumer lifecycle, when these systems gain traction and mature. T3 Sixty will continue monitoring this trend.

Lead Contributors:

Ben Clarke
Ben has a thirty-year career with companies such eRealty.com, Zillow and national home search platforms integrating affiliated mortgage solutions such as RocketHomes. Currently he works as a Strategist for real estate brokers and affinity programs looking to reduce the friction and cost in homebuying and selling. Ben can be reached at pbclark@gmail.com.

Jeremy Conaway
Jeremy is President of RECON Intelligence Services. He provides strategic design services and is currently focused on assisting traditional brokerages to transition to the Management Empowered Brokerage model as outlined in the 2018 Swanepoel Trends Report. Jeremy can be reached at jeremy.conaway@reconis.com.

SP200

Lookout for the 2019 Swanepoel Power 200 scheduled for release on Tuesday, January 15, 2019.

sp200.com
t360.com

Joan Docktor, President, BHHS Fox & Roach Realtors

From the Frontlines

- **What are the chief industry changes that affect your brokerage today?**

   The new entrants in the market bring a new flavor to the business. Change is happening at a faster pace than ever. We must provide our agents with best-of-breed tools and resources to help them prosper in this new, rapidly changing environment.

- **What are you doing about those changes?**

   We are upgrading our tech suite this fall (2018). We will have a new website and intranet from Reliance Network, a new CRM from Contactually, an engaging listing alert system from RealScout, and real estate data analytics from Buyside. We will continue to use the digital transaction management platform DocuSign Transaction Rooms. The way it will tie all these tools, as well as the way we and our agents will use them, will improve our performance and help us stand out.

   The integrated platform will make our agents more effective and help them do more business. For example, based on our test, Contactually emails have higher open rates. On the transaction side, DocuSign serves as a one-stop transaction hub where our agents and their clients as well as mortgage, title and insurance professionals can upload files and execute them with e-signatures.

   Purchasing technology allows us to be nimble – we can change course and evolve with new tools when they become available, rather than remain stuck with a system we built. We are not a technology company. Plenty of good tech companies exist. We will remain a HomeServices company. That is where our expertise lies.

   This nimble tech philosophy mirrors our office strategy — we do not buy our office buildings, but lease instead. We can shift and expand when opportune and contract, and adapt when circumstances change.

- **What are the biggest changes to your brokerage you have on the books for 2019? Why?**

   Rolling out our tech platform and, more importantly, getting agents to adopt it. We also recently hired the Ritz-Carlton to improve the service level of our staff. We aim to provide white-glove service to our agents and are training our staff accordingly.

- **What keeps you up at night as a brokerage leader?**

   Traditional real estate brokerage is an interesting business. We have independent contractors working for us. Agents have a choice whether to come back in the morning, so we must constantly prove our value to them. I worry now about what I always have — serving our agents as they want to be served. This is tricky.

   The business has changed over the years. Fewer agents are doing more of the business.

   We must attract agents and teams of all sizes. Agents attract their sphere of influence, the clients and customers. We would struggle to attract customers on our own, as that is not our business model. We must serve our agents, remain flexible and satisfy their ever-changing needs.

- **How are you outperforming newer brokerage business models?**

   We have been here 132 years and we expect to

be here another 132 years. Our longevity with deep roots in the local community gives us a huge advantage. As we all know, real estate is local. We have earned the trust of agents and consumers over decades.

But it is not just longevity. We are trusted advisors and we have always been and always will be on the cutting edge in our business. We do three times the business of our nearest competitor in most of our markets. That market size gives us a huge advantage.

HomeServices of America (HSA) bought our firm in 2013, but we still have local leadership. The relationship with HSA has given us incredible support as we share best practices and business intelligence with other brokerage leaders in the HSA family.

Real estate is a relationship business. Our agents' relationships are their lifeblood. Most will tell you that a majority of their business comes from their sphere of influence. Everything we do centers on helping them improve and strengthen those relationships.

- **Where do you think newer models have an edge? What are you doing about them?**

    Compass came into our market in June 2018 and, like they have done elsewhere, is buying agents. Discounters Redfin and Houwzer are also here. This forces us to up our game, and competition is good. We are better for it. We always have and continue to focus on developing tools for our agents. This includes assisting our agents with high-quality consumer marketing materials.

    We will always strive to improve. We are not going to stay where we are. I believe the competition makes us better and forces us to look at things differently.

    We focus on providing deep support to sales agents, which discounters cannot match. We have non-selling office leaders and admins who handle paperwork for our sales agents for no extra fee. Agents just need to be in front of their clients. We take care of all the administrative work. With our one-stop model, the transaction goes smoothly and we get their clients to the closing table.

    Real estate is a tough, litigious business and having full broker support behind our agents, and letting them know this, is one way we aim to stand out from more limited service models.

- **What do you see as the biggest long-term threat to your business?**

    I think some of the portals pose a threat. Zillow Group acquiring a mortgage company and getting a broker's license is concerning. Brokers have not watched these companies closely enough. I think consumers will always want a trusted advisor to assist them with what often is the biggest transaction of their life.

- **What do you think will be your firm's biggest differentiator in 2020?**

    The same as it is now. We have seen success and become market leaders because of our deep roots, and the trust and admiration we earn from our agents. We will remain on the cutting edge. We do not think that will change. enough. I think consumers will always want a trusted advisor to assist them with what often is the biggest transaction of their life.

Docktor joined Berkshire Hathaway HomeServices Fox & Roach as an agent in 1986, became general manager in 2003 and president in 2012. Founded in 1886, Berkshire Hathaway HomeServices Fox & Roach is one of the nation's oldest brokerages. It has 5,000 agents in 60 offices throughout the Delaware Valley, who do more than $11.7 billion in annual sales. Brokerage giant HomeServices of America acquired it in 2013. In addition to brokerage services, it offers mortgage, title insurance, property and casualty insurance under its Trident family of companies.

06 The NAR-Broker Relationship

How Brokerages Can Best Leverage NAR

Residential real estate brokerages and the National Association of Realtors have a long-standing, complicated and dynamic relationship. The massive shift underway in the industry rocks both brokerages and NAR and puts their relationship in flux. As brokerages strive to be more competitive and adapt to new technology and evolving consumer demands, NAR also seeks to remain relevant, provide value and communicate effectively with brokerages, but its a challenge for both.

This chapter outlines the NAR-brokerage relationship: where it is strong, where it is weak and how brokerage leaders can gain a deeper understanding of how they can leverage this powerful organization to improve their businesses and the industry at large.

How NAR Supports Brokerages

NAR works vigorously to protect the residential real estate brokerage industry and its broker and agent members through political advocacy, lobbying and by supporting the brokerage industry infrastructure itself. In many ways, NAR makes real estate brokerage possible, at least in its current form. It sets standards, guides industry policy and, in general, strives to make the industry as healthy as it can be for its members: brokers, agents and related real estate professionals.

NAR has a diverse mix of stakeholder groups, but the brokerage community is one of its largest and most critical. In many ways, as its relationship with brokers goes, so goes its relationship with the industry.

As a vital NAR partner, brokers typically set the direction of Realtor membership for their agents. In this way, they play a key role in supporting the association's large membership, which in 2018 stands at over 1.3 million real estate agents.

Directly and indirectly, the association supports the business of brokers and protects it in various ways. Much of what NAR does for the brokerage community runs in the background, establishing a productive landscape for the brokerage business. This close and dynamic relationship has many touchpoints; some of the most prominent are presented below.

NAR Direct Broker Support

Multiple Listing Services
There is no better-known or more-used asset in brokers' toolsets than the MLS. While the promotion of regulatory policy, professional standards and legal guidance are primary NAR member benefits for brokers, brokers and agents directly use the MLS more frequently than anything else NAR touches.

Most MLSs are owned by a local Realtor association, multiple associations or a broker-association conglomerate. Regardless of the structure, whether brokers and agents recognize it or not, the MLS is a primary benefit of Realtor membership. It serves as the glue that holds the residential real estate marketplace together.

Education
From the national organization to state and local Realtor associations, education is a large component of the relationship between NAR and real estate professionals. Realtor association instructors licensed by the state often teach accredited continuing education courses, ranging from those focused on the Realtor Code of Ethics to specialty

> "NAR is still the most valuable century-old asset in our industry."
>
> Stefan Swanepoel

designations. These instructors are often the most prominent direct interaction brokers and agents have with NAR. This education provides a valuable service to brokerages, especially those without extensive training and education departments.

Technology
NAR has focused on technology and product development in recent years with mixed success. It directly developed products such as SentriLock (sentrilock.com) and Realtors Property Resource (RPR, narrpr.com), invested in others through its for-profit Second Century Ventures subsidiary, and served as a service provider exemplified by RPR's role as developer of Project Upstream (upstreamre.com). Brokers have a mixed view of these efforts (more on their perceptions of NAR tech efforts below).

Smaller brokerages tend to appreciate NAR's efforts to supply technology their agents can use. Many also view it as a bulwark against a perceived threat of large tech companies and other firms from outside the industry, with massive amounts of funding. Some larger brokers chafe at NAR's tech efforts, preferring to provide technology to their agents themselves.

Research
NAR gathers data from many sources and produces industry-leading data to brokerages and agents. Its economic forecasting and homebuyer and homeseller research is widely acclaimed. Many brokerages use these to assess trends and develop strategy.

NAR research departments include consumer, economics and housing trends, which produce high-quality information for broker members. These reports are often broad, statistics-laden reports, which brokers and agents are often left to analyze and interpret themselves.

Legal Guidance
Brokers widely recognize NAR as their source for the most comprehensive legal guidance on general real estate issues. Timely updates on industry, legislative and regulatory changes are some of the most acutely understood and valued services the association provides. Whether from the national association's legal hotline or staff attorneys at state and local associations, this liability protection and support is a major resource for brokerages.

Forms
The association provides the legal guidance and organizational umbrella that supports the use of standardized forms across markets, in some cases statewide. Brokers value these standardized forms and recognize them as a significant NAR-provided asset.

Broker-NAR Relationship

Residential real estate brokerages and the National Association of Realtors have a long-standing, complicated and dynamic relationship. Below are the types of support NAR provides brokerages and the overall support brokers have for it.

National Association of Realtors Services

	Fundamental Service	Direct Service	Indirect Service
Strong Support	Advocacy	Education	MLS
		Research	
		Networking	Standards
		Legal	
Mild Support	Professionalism	Technology	Second Century Ventures
		Forms	REach

Level of Support from Brokers

Source: T3 Sixty

Events

Tens of thousands of Realtors interact with NAR directly at events each year. The most well-known are NAR's Annual Realtors Conference and Expo held every November, and the Realtors Legislative Meetings and Expo (commonly known as Midyear), held each May.

NAR has recently increased its focus on smaller, brokerage-focused events such as the Broker's Edge Event and Realtor Broker Summit. These are typically held at smaller venues in cities that do not often host large national conferences. They sell out quickly, but so far have been sparsely scheduled.

Building, Facilitating Coalition

NAR also facilitates invite-only broker meetings, which bring together the nation's largest brokers during NAR's national events, to discuss current industry issues. The best known of these are the Real Estate Services and Top 75 meetings. Topics at these meetings include major concerns of brokers big and small, such as protecting listing data, relationships with MLSs, and legislative, tax and regulatory issues.

NAR often pays for and organizes these events, while brokers lead and conduct the meetings themselves. In this way, NAR plays a third-party role in bringing the industry's broker power players together to strategize, discuss major issues and facilitate collaboration and communication.

More recently, NAR has attempted to bring brokerage and MLS executives together. MLS-broker relations have been contentious at times, and brokers continue to focus on MLSs in their effort to improve industry innovation. In 2016, NAR and the Council of Multiple Listing Services (councilofmls.org), announced a cooperative agreement aimed to increase operational collaboration between both groups.

NAR Indirect Broker Support

Much of the way NAR supports the brokerage community runs in the background; in short, it establishes the framework for the residential real estate brokerage business. These services might be the most financially valuable to brokerages, but can be difficult to quantify.

Advocacy and Lobbying

Several volumes could be written on the breadth of the advocacy efforts and campaigns managed by NAR year in and year out. The successes are celebrated on a regular basis and the association's clout in Washington, D.C., is without question. In addition, NAR's support for individual property rights is second to none.

> "Several volumes could be written on the breadth of the advocacy efforts and campaigns managed by NAR."

NAR's success surrounding 2018's tax reform legislation provides an example of its significant lobbying power. It helped reverse nearly all proposed legislation that would have hampered the industry. For example, it helped prevent a limit on who could claim a capital gain tax exclusion on a home sale; a proposal would have required homeowners to live in a home five of the past eight years to be eligible for the tax exclusion rather than two of the past five years. This would have increased the tax hit many sellers face on a home sale.

Consumer Advocacy

NAR markets the Realtor brand directly to consumers through digital, print and TV advertising. Sometimes these efforts focus on the difference between Realtor and non-Realtor licensees, while others simply emphasize the value of using a real estate professional when buying or selling a home. These campaigns have received scrutiny recently as some brokers question their efficacy and prefer NAR focus its efforts on activities that more directly support their businesses. On the other hand, a significant portion of membership vigorously lobbies for these consumer marketing campaigns.

Industry Standards

One of NAR's greatest assets is its role as a broker-neutral industry advocate. Brokers of all sizes ask the association to help set standards, rules, MLS IDX policy and minimum, core standards for local and state associations. NAR's support for orderly brokerage cooperation and competition through the MLS standards and policy help create stable real estate marketplaces that brokerages enjoy throughout the US. Compliance for local association standards, however, sometimes creates friction between local associations and their brokers.

Real Estate Standards Organization

While no longer a NAR entity, the Real Estate Standards Organization (RESO, reso.org) was created by NAR and and has also been supported by it financially. RESO develops data standards that help facilitate collaboration among brokerages, MLSs and other players. For more on RESO, see Trend No. 5.

MLS and IDX Policy

NAR's model policies for MLSs and how they distribute data help improve the industry's technology systems. Multi-market brokers have struggled with disjointed and confusing technology solutions since listings first went online. By outlining a standard policy for sharing and displaying listings for brokerages in markets across the nation, NAR helps support efficient, new and competitive ways of sharing data.

Core Standards for Associations

When NAR adopted core standards requirements for associations in

2014, it demanded that every local association deliver a minimum set of benefits to member brokers and agents, such as political advocacy, consumer outreach, outlining member benefits on a website and operating in a fiscally responsible manner. This spurred some associations to merge and others to improve.

Small brokers benefited from these standards as some paid dues to associations with no full-time staff and few services to offer. Earnest as these association leaders were, they simply could not meet the needs of their members. The core standards initiative by NAR has helped improve association services, ensuring small brokers in remote locations receive clear benefits from their local associations.

Professionalism Efforts and the Code of Ethics

Professionalism is a core component of NAR's mission and is a large part of why the organization came into existence — a lawless, unscrupulous industry at the turn of the twentieth century needed rules, regulations and consumer protections to establish residential real estate as a reputable trade.

NAR's Code of Ethics outlines how members should conduct their business. Brokers can register complaints about other members who violate the professional code through local associations; violators can face penalties. Essential to establishing nationwide standards, the Code is highly revered by engaged membership. Yet, it is hardly a secret that the penalty enforcement system remains underutilized, which hampers its ability to improve market-wide professionalism.

Second Century Ventures and REach Technology Accelerator
NAR's for-profit strategic investment subsidiary Second Century Ventures (SCV, secondcenturyventures.com) invests in real estate technology companies it believes will benefit Realtor practitioners. In 2018, the fund realized a big return when DocuSign, in which it invested in 2009, went public. SCV sold 28 percent of its shares for a $43.8 million windfall. SCV transferred $20 million to NAR to recoup its initial investment and added the balance to its fund for further investment.

Second Century Ventures also runs a technology accelerator, REach (narreach.com), which it launched in 2013. Designed to help startups connect with the real estate industry, the accelerator helps cultivate broker-friendly technology that benefits the industry. In some cases, such as DocuSign (docusign.com), it helps guide the development of leading, industry-changing technologies. In summer 2018, REach had fifty companies in its portfolio including DocuSign, realtor.com operator Move Inc. and RealScout (realscout.com).

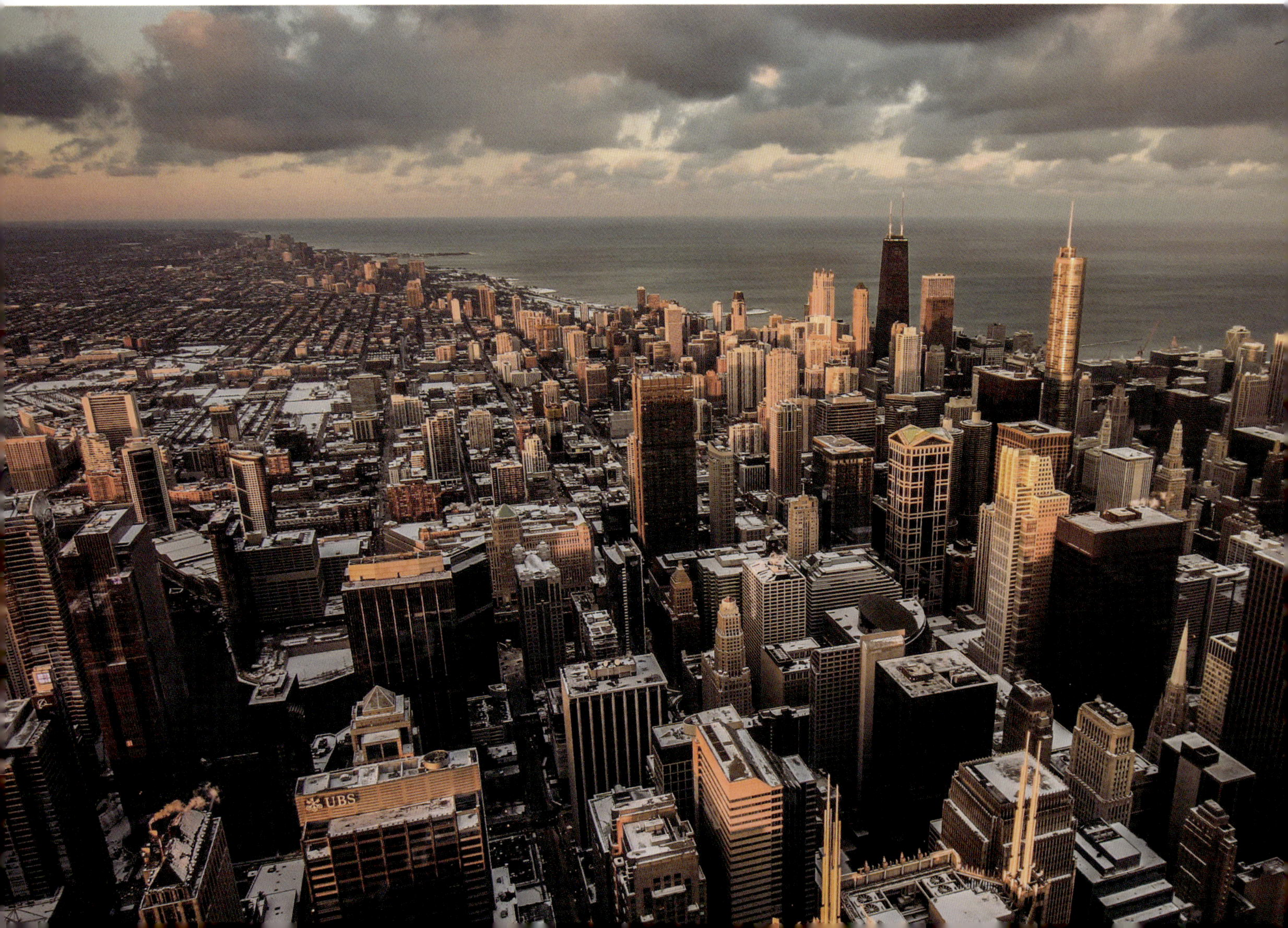

Chief Areas of Relationship Strain

As outlined above, NAR supports brokerages in multiple ways. While the industry tends to constantly have gripes with the association, many have an overall positive view of it, especially when it comes to their excellent lobbying, advocacy and government affairs work.

Brokers are a diverse lot and their feelings toward NAR, of course, differ. Brokerage concerns range from NAR's involvement in funding and developing industry technology to its consumer marketing campaigns. Brokerages' feelings about these hot-button issues often split based on their size.

Some large brokers dislike NAR advertising Realtors to consumers, as they believe it is an ineffectual exercise and use of funds. Many larger brokers also do not appreciate the organization building technology as they prefer to handle that themselves for their agents. They feel better equipped to do it, and want to provide that value to agents and leverage it as a competitive advantage. Smaller brokers, on the other hand, tend to appreciate technology that helps their agents, which they do not have the scale to offer themselves.

In addition, some NAR-provided technology, such as ZipLogix, is not available in all markets, which aggravates brokers and agents in those markets as their dues dollars go to a benefit they cannot use. Some of the areas where brokerages have concerns are outlined below.

Spending

Brokerages, in many ways, are on the frontline representing NAR to their agents. Brokers choose their Realtor affiliation and their agents must follow suit (if they do not, brokers must pay their member dues).

When NAR spends money in seemingly controversial ways, brokers take the heat from their agents, who pay annual dues of $120 to be members in 2018 (dues go up to $150 in 2019). RPR is one example. When it launched in 2009, it was said the technology would be profitable and generate large streams of revenue for NAR. But RPR has generated losses of nearly $180 million through the beginning of 2018, despite repeated forecasts that profitability was just around the corner.

Technology

While some NAR-backed products have facilitated much-needed industry competition such as SentriLock (see the sidebar in this chapter for more details) and viewed by brokerages positively, brokers see others as unnecessary, unproductive ventures.

RPR

RPR (narrpr.com) gives NAR members access to data on 166 million properties in the US, including access to market activity, sellers, property and neighborhood reports. Brokerages who have built their own backoffice tools to create customized reports for their agents, though, sometimes view RPR as unnecessary. In addition, brokerages in areas where RPR cannot access important data and therefore is not useful, resent their agents' dues going toward a tool they do not benefit from.

ZipLogix

Since 2015, NAR has provided a basic version of the full zipLogix transaction management platform (zipLogix.com) as a benefit to its Realtor members (zipLogix makes the popular real estate forms software zipForms). NAR pays approximately $12 million per year to zipLogix as a part of the agreement.

While brokers and their agents appreciate access to a free tool, many have some concerns with the deal. First, brokers in markets where zipForms are not used do not benefit from the technology. Second, while zipLogix is a free member benefit, critical components of the platform are not included in the free version, including its mobile app and e-signature capability, two huge features of any modern digital platform. Another concern some brokers have with the zipLogix offering is that they prefer, and pay for, alternative platforms whose price points and functionality rival that of zipLogix' full platform. In effect, these brokers and their agents pay a premium for transaction management — they pay for their preferred platform and for zipLogix, which they do not use.

ZipLogix' ownership structure also complicates the deal for some brokers. The structure is a joint venture between NAR and the California Association of Realtors subsidiary Real Estate Business Services Inc. (REBS). As a result, zipLogix has close ties to the association world, leaving some brokers feeling that NAR's investment in a tech it owns muddies the water. The fact that some question whether zipLogix is the best transaction management tool to provide as a member benefit and whether another should have been chosen, if any, adds to the friction.

ZipLogix ownership breaks down as follows: NAR owns 30.2 percent, REBS owns 57.4 percent, zipLogix owns 11.6 percent and a handful of other state and local Realtor associations own the remaining 0.8 percent.

Realtor.com

After flying high in the mid-nineties realtor.com (holding company at the time was HomeStore) experienced a rocky road when in 2002, then CEO Stuart Wolff was sued for issuing misleading financial statements. Wolff eventually served four and a half years in federal prison. Homestore rebranded to Move Inc. in 2006 and was subsequently acquired in 2014 by global media giant News Corp. for $950 million. An amended version of the 1996 operating agreement inked with HomeStore licensing the Realtor brand is still in effect.

How NAR Can Bring More Value To Brokerages

Bob Goldberg

NAR's mission is multipronged, ranging from advocacy to professionalism, research, legal guidance, business tools and technology. From national campaigns to improve professionalism to direct consumer advertising, NAR has a full plate. While NAR can support all these initiatives, it might gain most by focusing on a few achievable, valuable and relevant benefits for brokers.

While strengthening its value for the brokerage community is a complex venture, the basic tenets of improving broker support are straightforward. By focusing on the services that brokerages cannot or will not provide for themselves, NAR can help brokerages immensely. NAR is in a unique position to bring brokerages together, to facilitate collaboration and organize brokerage knowledge, services and tools at a scale no other entity can.

Some areas where NAR can help brokers include:

- Negotiating scale-based cost savings with popular companies. If NAR can negotiate competitive rates for a popular service, brokers will benefit directly.

- Helping brokers get involved in lobbying and advocating for issues important to the industry and their local markets. In addition to the work it does directly, NAR has the clout and expertise to guide brokers in supporting government policies that help them at both the national and local level.

- Facilitating cooperation and communication among brokerages to help them strategize and mastermind about important issues that will help them succeed in a fast-changing industry. NAR already does this to some extent, but it could do even more.

- Making a push to process and analyze industry data not available anywhere else. This is a daunting task, given many brokers' and MLSs' wariness to share data with anyone else, but is potentially extremely beneficial, especially as big data becomes an ever more important technological asset.

- Investing more in Second Century Ventures and REach. By introducing promising innovators to the Realtor brand and guiding them to build products that solve broker needs, NAR can be an even more effective broker technology partner.

- Highlighting the legal guidance resources NAR tailors for brokers. These resources can fly under the radar, but are immensely valuable and should be featured.

What New NAR Leadership Means For Brokers

Under new CEO Bob Goldberg, NAR has announced various changes, and is already restructuring the organization to be more responsive to

membership. NAR has merged departments to streamline communication and operations, and combined related parts of the organization in research, technology and communications.

Changes to NAR Structure

NAR's traditional structure contributed to some of the disconnect between NAR, brokers and other constituents. It is no surprise that with 1.3 million members, successful engagement on a broad scale is a difficult task. To improve communication, NAR is restructuring individual departments to make them more nimble and responsive. The four that have changed most dramatically and primarily affect the NAR-brokerage relationship are covered below.

Marketing, Communications and Events

NAR has merged these previously separate divisions into one group under NAR Senior Vice President Matt Lombardi. While NAR has always provided robust content and events marketing, the need to tailor communications to brokers is clear. Engaging brokers in its value proposition is a focus for NAR, and the new combined division is already at work. For example, the group highlighted NAR's 2018 budget process and dues increase in town halls, webinars and detailed live videos at a volume and speed not seen before. Reports directly from the organization minutes after its board of directors or leadership team makes decisions illustrate a new focus NAR has of communicating directly with membership.

Political Advocacy

In 2018, long-time NAR lobbyist Jerry Giovanello retired after twenty-eight years of service. Shannon Flaherty McGahn, married to former Trump Administration White House Counsel Don McGahn, has filled the post.

Earlier in 2018, NAR appointed Bill Malkasian to Senior Vice President and Chief Advocacy Officer. NAR has a new team to continue its strong relationships in Washington with regulatory agencies, the US Congress and the White House.

Research

The association has also integrated its Market Research team, Predictive Analytics team and all other research divisions into a single division responsible for all data collection. Led by Senior Vice President and Chief Economist Lawrence Yun, this division plans to significantly broaden its research into external trends, consumer activity and membership data to provide holistic research and knowledge

for broker partners. This group will spearhead NAR's aim to deliver more analysis and data to the industry.

Strategic Business Innovation and Technology
The newly formed Strategic Business Innovation and Technology division combines the Center for Realtor Technology, Second Century Ventures, the REach accelerator, and multiple other technology initiatives into one. Under Senior Vice President Mark Birschbach, this group plans to expand its offerings significantly in the coming years to spur industry technology innovation that benefits members.

Change Challenges
NAR faces some institutional challenges when making changes. These include a 900-member board of directors, which many cite as an impediment to association innovation. Much like the US Congress, its large size helps prevent rash or erratic change, but also often hampers speed and innovation by making big, quick decisions and moves difficult.

> "The highest performing brokers and agents tend to focus most of their energy on their own businesses and not on NAR policy and structure."

Despite this structure, the association's leadership can make decisions and move the organization quickly, when necessary. But when it does, it must walk a tightrope between board of director members who prefer more thoughtful, measured action and those who want to move quickly.

The demographics of NAR's volunteer leadership can also slow innovation. NAR leaders tend to be long-term association volunteers who have put in their time to achieve important positions. The commitment required to rise through the ranks often means these Realtors are closer to the end of their career than the beginning. This leads to vast knowledge, experience and stability, but also, in some cases, to fixed states of mind and resistance to new technology and initiatives. These are mixed blessings for brokers.

In a rapidly shifting landscape, NAR leaders must have their eyes and minds wide open to ensure NAR adapts in ways that keep it relevant and useful to brokers and other members. The highest performing brokers and agents tend to focus most of their energy on their own businesses and not on NAR policy and structure. This leaves many of the sharpest, most knowledgeable member minds on the sidelines. Efforts to bring them into NAR decision-making processes can be beneficial for all involved.

Takeaway

When brokers and agents founded NAR in 1908, they were looking to professionalize their nascent industry. Today in 2018, 110 years later, both have matured into powerhouses.

As chronicled in this report, the continued evolution of technology, the massive amounts of outside capital being invested into new business models is fueling significant change in the industry. Massive change happens in every industry era, and NAR has in the past been a stable brokerage support that has helped brokers evolve through one cycle to another.

But this cycle is different. It is placing new pressure on the relationship between NAR and brokers, and moving it into unfamiliar territory.

Though sometimes an easy place for brokerages to levy their frustrations at NAR, NAR can be a valuable asset and brokerages have a lot to gain in leveraging their national organization as a powerful, strategic partner. Brokerages and and NAR need each other, perhaps now more than ever.

> "Brokerages and NAR need each other, perhaps now more than ever."

Lead Contributor:

Sam DeBord
Sam is Vice President of Strategic Growth for Coldwell Banker Danforth in Seattle. He is a frequent contributor to well-known industry news outlets, a consultant and facilitator for real estate and technology organizations, as well as 2019 NAR President's Liaison for MLS and Data Management issues. Sam can be reached at sam@seattlehome.com.

OB Jacobi, Co-President, Windermere Real Estate

From the Frontlines

 What are the chief industry changes that affect your brokerage today?

The shift from a completely agent-centric industry to one where agents see the benefits of co-branding with their brokerage. Some companies have allowed their agents to become almost completely autonomous, but in certain cases it went too far. Do not get me wrong, we believe that the agent should be front and center, but there certainly is a place for the brokerage, as well, and this is more apparent today than in years past.

We are in a time of amazing consolidation, driven by huge amounts of outside funding. Innovation just happens faster now. Ideas emerge and are executed in the blink of an eye. Real estate is an emotional, infrequent transaction. I do not see somebody coming along and fundamentally changing that.

New business models are entering the real estate space in the hopes of capturing the business that our agents have worked so hard to cultivate. When the market shifts, who knows if these new models will survive. Regardless, I know that brokerages that listen to the needs of their agents and adapt, will thrive.

We know the market is slowing, so we will see how much money stays in the industry. Everybody wants a piece when the market is thriving.

- **What are you doing about those changes?**

Windermere has always seen its role as building entrepreneurs. We are doubling down on that. Our agents today want more help managing their business. Instead of just pointing them to vetted vendors, our agents say they want us to manage those vendors on their behalf. Building your team and managing that team is tough and agents are relying on us more for that.

We are in the process of building an in-house marketing agency that supports several Windermere offices in the Seattle area. With this, our agents can focus on their business, while we find and vet quality marketing staff.

Agents of all production levels require some amount of outside support, but not everyone can afford — or needs — a full-time assistant. We are building support teams as a resource for our agents, so they can focus on their clients and not on managing a staff or mastering new technologies.

- **What are the biggest changes to your brokerage you have on the books for 2019? Why?**

Several Windermere office owners have come together in the Seattle area to build and pilot an in-house creative agency that provides services to about 1,400 agents. Once we develop and fine-tune the agency, we will offer the playbook to the rest of our franchise owners to implement it in their own offices.

Technology adoption is always a challenge, and we constantly work to improve it. We are developing new marketing platforms that make it simple for our agents, to promote their listing and themselves. We are also focused on improving our company website, agent websites, and training that allow our franchise owners and agents to be more efficient.

- **What keeps you up at night as a brokerage leader?**

    Everything! I monitor the new business models, but care most about our agents. I am constantly thinking about how we can better support our agents so they can have a semblance of balance in their lives. To us, work-life balance is a critical part of success. We talk about this early and often with our agents to ensure they have plans that will make them happy and healthy.

- **How are you outperforming newer brokerage business models?**

    A strong franchise network made up of owners deeply committed to their agents and their local communities is one of our biggest advantages. Our local owners cultivate individual relationships with their agents and encourage them to develop close relationships with their clients. We also promote a selling philosophy centered on working with people we know, like and trust.

    Our culture also stands out. For example, the Windermere Foundation, which raises about $2.4 million each year from our agents, donates to organizations that support low-income and homeless families. We are also one of the only real estate companies in the nation to offer our agents a retirement program.

    As the founder of Moxi Works, which we spun off as a separate firm in 2010, we also offer strong technology programs and tools. Moxi Works, which merges a CRM, intranet and email marketing into one platform, is recognized as one of the top tools of its kind in our industry and gives our agents a real competitive advantage.

- **Where do you think newer models have an edge? What are you doing about them?**

    I think the new models are telling a better story right now. They offer agents nothing fundamentally different than us, but they are making a big splash and agents are paying attention. We are working to retell our story in a way that resonates with agents and consumers.

- **What do you see as the biggest long-term threat to your business?**

    If Direct Buyers take transactions off the table that could have a big impact. I am not sure they are coming to higher-priced markets such as Seattle, but they will probably end up in some of our other markets. I am curious to see the types of transactions, price points and areas the model finds success in.

    Another looming threat is the immense technology, money, brand and consumer relationships that large companies such as Amazon, Google and Facebook have. If they jump into real estate, it could deeply shake the industry.

- **What do you think will be your firm's biggest differentiator in 2020?**

    Our differentiator is and always will be our people. That is the difference between us and the new companies entering our business. Our people are the fabric of their communities and that cannot be replaced by big money.

Jacobi guides business strategies for Windermere's franchise network and oversees the company's six family-owned offices along with his sister Jill Jacobi Wood. OB is son of Windermere founder John Jacobi. Windermere Real Estate has over 300 offices and 6,500 agents in ten western US states. In 2017, companies under the Windermere brand sold 84,000 homes for more than $36.3 billion in sales.

05 Real Estate Data Standards

What's Really Happening with RETS and Web API

Open real estate data standards underpin the competitive real estate technology marketplace the industry depends on. Nearly all of the real estate data coursing through industry websites and backend systems currently runs through RETS, which the industry has used to transmit and share data for nearly two decades. In recent years, the industry, through the nonprofit Real Estate Standards Organization (RESO), has worked to standardize data terms and fields through the Data Dictionary, and is developing a new way of transmitting data through a Web API.

In this chapter, T3 Sixty outlines the current real estate data standards landscape — where things stand, where they will head and why.

Understanding Real Estate Data Standards

> "I truly admire and adore our MLS and association leaders but also burn with frustration at how many slow-play meaningful change."
>
> Stefan Swanepoel

The real estate brokerage industry's primary producers and consumers of data include real estate brokerage companies and their agents, MLSs, MLS software vendors, and brokerage and agent technology vendors. These groups must be able to share information with each other in an easy, straightforward format. In addition, brokerages and their agents must be able to add and change content (primarily related to listings), and aggregate and search data.

Moving this data involves two key components: the data itself and the process by which it moves.

In real estate data standards parlance, the term *resource* refers to the data moved around. The term *transport* refers to how data moves — how software accesses the *resource*, queries it and what structure the returned information takes. Simply put, *transport* describes the mechanism used to move the *resource*. A rocket ship provides a good analogy: the *transport* is the ship itself and the *resource* is the payload the ship blasts into space.

Data Dictionary – Defining Real Estate's Resource

In 2010, RESO (reso.org) began work on the Data Dictionary, a national specification that establishes standard definitions for most MLS data resources and their fields. This standard streamlines the sharing and interpreting of data between brokerages and MLSs in multiple markets; historically, MLSs developed their own terms and definitions for common fields.

The Data Dictionary greatly improves data sharing as it defines a common language understandable by all. In other words, it optimizes real estate resources for transport.

The resource definitions in the current version of the Data Dictionary, version 1.6, include:

- **Property:** listings data, including all fields describing the listing.

- **Member:** an association or MLS member's profile and contact information.

- **Office:** a real estate office.

- **Contacts:** consumer contact information stored by an MLS member.

- **Media:** photographs and videos associated with listings.

- **History (Transactional):** a record of changes to data fields for any MLS resource, who changed them and when.

- **Saved Search:** a specific consumer's saved search preferences.

- **Open House:** an event associated with a listing, with a time and date stamp.

- **Teams and Team Members:** groups of agents that identify as a team, for listing- and sales-tracking purposes.

- **Organizational Unique Identifier:** a unique identifier for each technology vendor, MLS system, broker and anyone else that uses or exchanges data using the RESO standards.

When it comes out in late 2018, version 1.7 of the Data Dictionary, will define over 4,000 values, according to RESO. New definitions will include standards for the following fields: lockbox, membership, listing data business rules and days on market. Additional definitions will cover brokerage-specific fields related to listings, staff and agent rosters and offices.

Future Data Dictionary standards may make it easier for brokers to transition to new data systems, including transaction management platforms and CRMs. At this point, the standards and their implementation by technology vendors do not yet support this level of

Standards: Not Just an MLS Thing

Currently, most of the servers providing standardized real estate data belong to the MLS, but brokers should be advocating for — and contracting for — their technology providers to use the widely used standards, namely the Data Dictionary and the Web API. For example, if brokers want data beyond listings to efficiently flow from lead generation systems to CRMs, lead management platforms, marketing systems, websites and transaction management platforms, all the systems need to speak the same language. The RESO Data Dictionary defines that language. For the highest efficiency, broker and agent systems should send data from certified standards-compliant servers.

> "RETS is a transport the industry devised almost twenty years ago to handle real estate data."

plug-and-play functionality, as the Data Dictionary does not yet include the resource definitions to support it.

Transport

There are two protocols currently available to move real estate data: RETS (older format) and the Web API (newer format). RESO plays a key role in both. RESO has guided and supported RETS for years, but stopped supporting it in 2018 to focus its energies on the Web API.

RETS

The Real Estate Transaction Standard, which the industry knows as RETS, is a transport the industry devised almost twenty years ago to handle real estate data. It is based on the XML meta language for defining web documents and mark up. The RETS standard specifies the particular way systems can query and retrieve real estate data from MLSs and other systems.

After replacing the cumbersome, fragile FTP method, RETS has served as the mainstay of real estate industry data transport for nearly two decades. It is unique to real estate; no other industry uses the standard to transport data.

Most real estate applications today use RETS to query the MLS, download MLS data for reuse (also known as replication) and share data with other systems. RETS can also be used to conduct real-time queries for more transient use, such as pulling a handful of listing fields for display.

Web API

In 2013, RESO, MLSs and technology providers began working on a new standards specification for transport known as Web API, which incorporates global standards common to most industries. For example, instead of using the RETS login process that only exists inside the real estate industry, the Web API standard leverages Oauth and OpenID Connect standards, used by technology companies and developers throughout the world.

The Web API also leverages multi-industry standards such as JSON, ATOM/XML and OData. Programmers around the world learn about these standards in school or have used them at work. The Web API has made great strides in 2018, but still needs to evolve. The current version 1.0.3 does not include specifications for the following actions, in RESO's words (with T3 Sixty's comments in parentheses):

- Create, Update, Delete resource content (current release is read only)
- A Data Replication Framework (features for synchronizing data are not available)
- Requesting Binary Media Resources (downloading images is not supportedvia the API)
- Updating Binary Media Resources (uploading images is not supported)
- Saved Searches and Resources (these resource types are not yet supported)

These limitations are not unworkable and some of them also exist with RETS.

> " The Web API has made great strides in 2018, but still needs to evolve."

What Makes The Web API Better

When fully functional, the new Web API transport protocol will not offer significant advantages over RETS. Data will move nearly exactly the same as it does with RETS; storage requirements and security remain largely unchanged as well.

RETS is not terribly difficult or time-consuming for developers to learn but the Web API does ease the barrier to entry for developers not already in real estate and therefore may bring more innovation to the industry.

As a lighter-weight transport standard, the Web API should also support faster speeds for mobile applications. Perhaps most importantly, the new transport protocol will support future cross-industry integrations with mortgage, title, insurance and other key industries adjacent to residential real estate.

NAR'S Role

To help spur the industry's move to more contemporary, useful standards, NAR required that all Realtor-affiliated MLSs adopt the RESO Web API standard by July 1, 2016. Initially, a majority of the nation's 700 MLSs did not comply, which compelled NAR to threaten removing NAR-provided E&O (errors and omissions) insurance if Realtor-owned MLSs did not adopt the standards.

With the NAR-spurring policy helping inspire action, now nearly two-thirds of the nation's current 623 MLSs (as of mid-2018) are certified on the RESO Web API, according to RESO. Separately, 95 percent of MLSs are currently certified on the RESO Data Dictionary, another crucial component to moving the industry ahead.

In mid-2018, RESO certified real estate data partners separately on Data Dictionary and Web API standards. However, in 2019, RESO expects to require that all real estate data transmitted through the Web API comply with the Data Dictionary. It will eventually marry these two standards together as a condition of certification and compliance with RESO standards.

Fact Checking

T3 Sixty uncovered some common Web API misunderstandings in its research. Some of them are presented below.

Replication

Brokers have perhaps heard that RETS requires replicating data, that systems must copy data from one database to another, while the Web API supports transient download, where systems access data at the source only when they need it.

Both RETS and the Web API can be used to replicate data or access data in real time through transient download. In fact, a replication framework for the Web API is currently in the works to make it easier for data users to copy an MLS database.

Many, possibly most, applications naturally require replication, regardless of the transport protocol used. Any application that analyzes big data or trains an artificial intelligence system will replicate a database

> "Transporting data through RETS, the Web API or any other protocol does not change the role of the MLS as data gatekeeper."

— pulling data from a data source just when needed would prove wildly inefficient.

Similarly, broker and agent IDX websites will not likely pull listings down from the MLS to regenerate their listing detail pages every time a consumer searches for a property; they will replicate the database instead. Of course, transient download makes sense in some cases; but most real estate applications require full database replication. This will continue with the Web API.

Security and API

Some brokers may hear that the Web API provides better security as data users do not need to replicate databases as often under the protocol. As explained above, this is not true. Both protocols support replication and transient download and those needs will not change with a new transport protocol. Data is not more secure with the Web API than with RETS.

It might surprise many to learn that RETS is actually an API, too. It just uses protocols specific to the residential real estate brokerage industry.

MLS Role

Some may hear that the Web API protocol will allow data to flow more freely between industry participants outside of MLS control or will make the MLS role as data conduit more efficient. Transporting data through RETS, the Web API or any other protocol does not change the role of the MLS as data gatekeeper. The same licensing and controls currently in place remain the same regardless of how the data moves.

Offering the Web API

Not every MLS or data provider offers the Web API — but T3 Sixty thinks it is important that all industry data players do, along with certified compliant versions of the Data Dictionary and, at least for now, RETS.

NAR mandated that NAR-affiliated MLSs had to start offering the Web API in 2016, so Realtor association-affiliated MLSs not offering a Web API feed to their brokers are out of compliance.

Some think that MLSs should force all their technology providers and their member's technology providers to use the Web API within the next year. This is unrealistic and potentially anticompetitive.

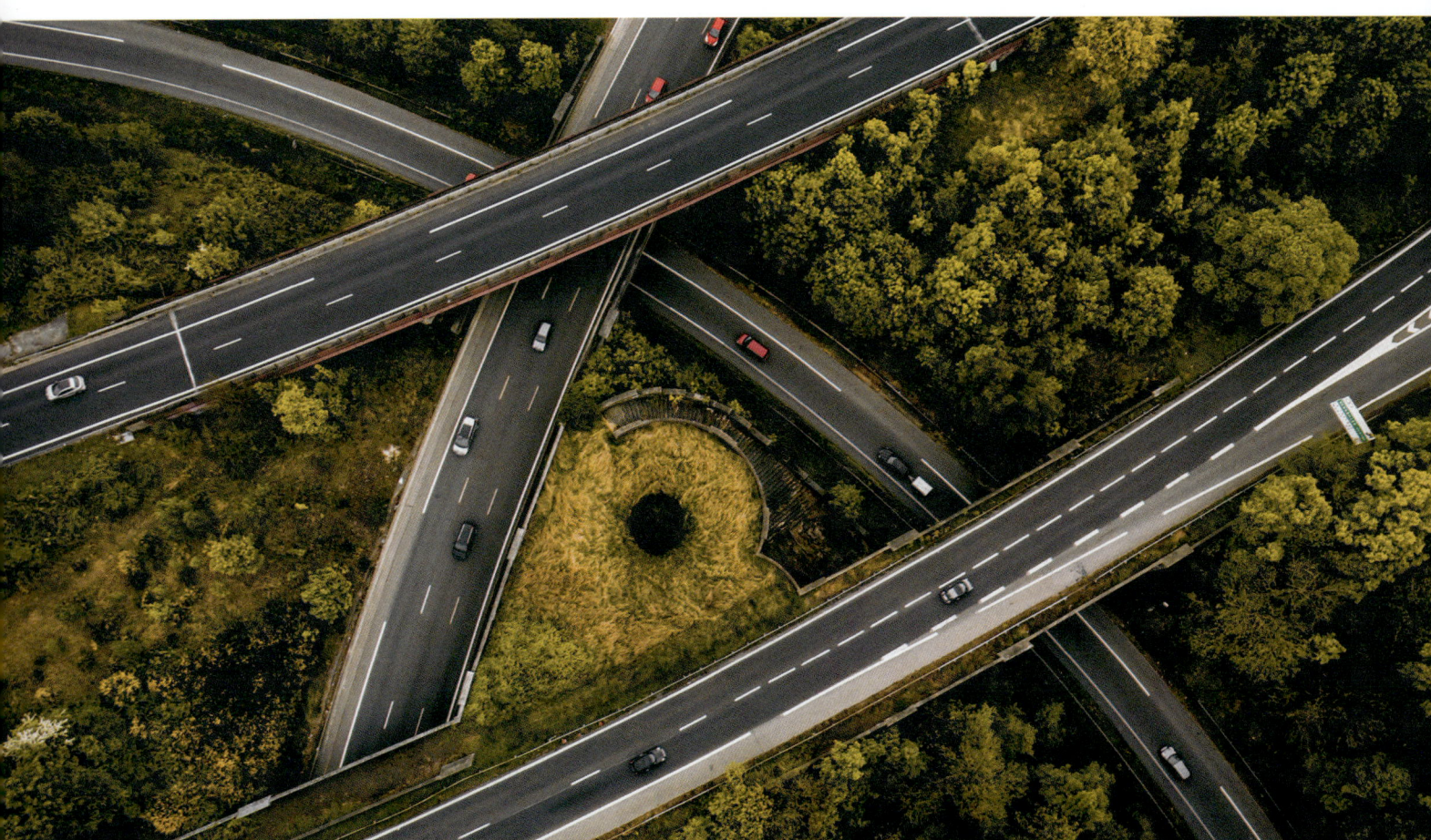

> "The Web API will potentially enable cross-industry integrations with mortgage, title, insurance and other key industries adjacent to residential real estate."

Many thousands of smaller technology providers leverage the RETS transport today and may find it financially burdensome to make a change in a short period of time. If technology providers only offer websites to a few agents or brokers in an MLS, and if they try to pass on the cost of making the Web API change to their customers, the MLS could face pushback. If the MLSs hold firm, those providers might go out of business and leave their subscribers scrambling for other technology solutions, or potentially inspire an anticompetitive suit.

New industry vendors should choose the Web API. The market will do some of the work in transitioning the industry from RETS to the Web API. When MLSs offer both feeds — RETS and the Web API — the vendors using the Web API might outcompete those using RETS, if it proves to be that much better. At that point, vendors will migrate to the new standard or go out of business.

Brokers must work together to voice their support of the new standard and then demand their MLSs keep up and modernize. New and existing technology providers should be encouraged to use the Web API to transport data and make the investments necessary to do so.

Roughly two-thirds of the nation's 623 MLSs have 1,000 or fewer subscribers. Many smaller MLSs do not have the resources or skills to help facilitate a migration from RETS to the Web API. In these cases, their leadership and constituents need to explore other strategies such as consolidating or joining a larger MLS data group.

> "Brokers must work together to voice their support of the new standard and then demand their MLSs keep up and modernize."

Takeaway

While the new data transport system, Web API, offers some near-term advantages, they are not game-changing. RETS still works and thousands of companies currently depend on it to share and transmit real estate data every day. As such, RETS will remain as a real estate transport option for at least a few more years.

MLSs and brokerages should encourage Web API development and convince any colleagues skittish about its potential to bring new competition to let this mindset go. True competition will always come down to executing on service, brand and technology and not to an industry-exclusive software or outdated gatekeeper role.

As the industry's primary data hub, MLSs have a central role in moving the industry to the new Web API. The steps they should take include:

- MLSs that do not yet comply with RESO standards must set a target date to offer RESO-compliant Web API and Data Dictionary feeds in 2019. Every MLS must do this to start the ball rolling with technology providers and brokerages.

- Every MLS should broadcast their support for the Web API and plan to phase out RETS and communicate the phase-out to membership and data partners in monthly written messages.

- RESO and MLSs should highlight innovative RESO-compliant solutions that serve brokers and other data users and depend on the Web API and Data Dictionary to function.

- MLSs should require all new vendors use the Web API.

While MLSs have a more immediate role in transitioning the industry to its new data standards, brokers play a critical part, too. They should demand that their MLSs adopt the Web API and provide compliant feeds that work. If left only to MLSs and their software provider, the transition will take much longer.

Lead Contributors:

Paul Hagey
Paul is Executive Editor of the *Swanepoel Trends Report*, founding Publisher of Boulder, Colorado, magazine BLDRfly and runs the content agency HageyMedia. He began covering the real estate in-dustry as fulltime reporter with Inman News, where he became an award-winning journalist. Paul is a graduate of the University of Missouri Graduate School of Journalism. Paul can be reached at paul@t360.com.

Jack Miller
Jack has two decades of experience in the real estate industry and today serves as the President and CTO of T3 Sixty, where he heads up their consulting team. He previously worked as CTO of the Austin, Texas-based boutique brokerage The GoodLife Team, and prior to that he led a technology team with Keller Williams Realty. Jack can be reached at jack@t360.com.

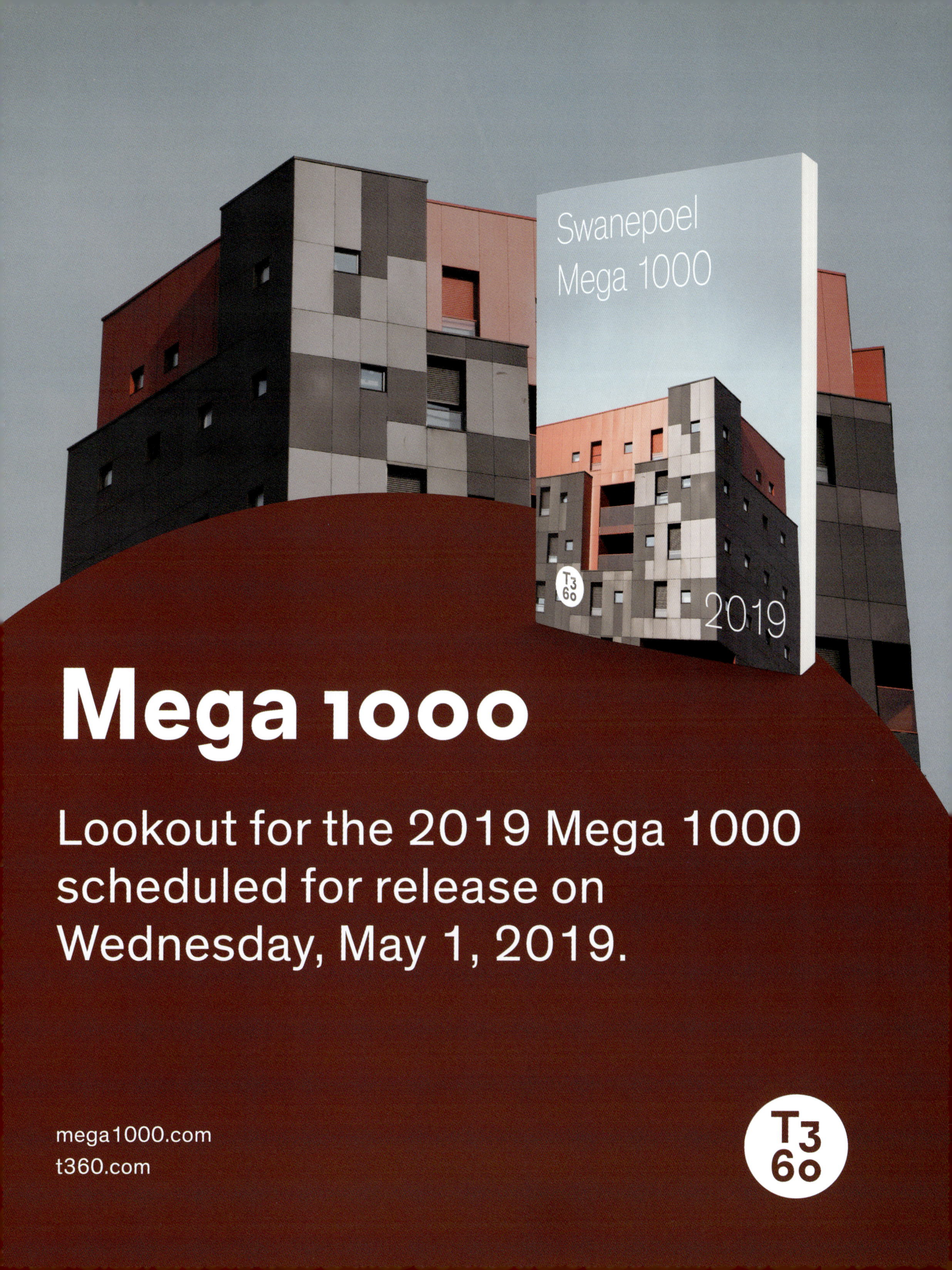

Mega 1000

Lookout for the 2019 Mega 1000 scheduled for release on Wednesday, May 1, 2019.

mega1000.com
t360.com

Paul Breunich, President and Owner, William Pitt-Julia B. Fee Sotheby's International Realty

From the Frontlines

- **What are the chief industry changes that affect your brokerage today?**

  Technology has been driving industry change for five or six years and the rate of change is rapidly increasing thanks to newer business models and consumers pushing the envelope. Outside funding is shaking up the industry. Many companies are receiving large equity infusions, which create unbalanced short-term market conditions. That being said, competition is good. It makes us all better.

- **What are you doing about those changes?**

  Our approach has always been, and will continue to be, highly proactive. We keep our ears to the ground and adapt to the ever-changing industry. If you have not been innovating over the past eight years, you should be sweating.

  One area where we are innovating is our website. Four years ago, we felt that our platform was not delivering what we needed, so we set out to design and build a brand new site. This year, Real Trends recognized it as the country's best overall real estate site.

  We are also replacing our backend system with an all-in-one platform that is being designed to meet every conceivable need of today's real estate professional, and seamlessly integrate with other tools and technology we have found to be effective. The new tech platform launches in April 2019, and it is all hands on deck to get there. Competition adds fuel to the fire.

  Agent retention and recruiting is becoming a battleground. We have always emphasized strong communication with our agents, and we strive to cultivate trust through transparency by providing a window into the thought process behind our business decisions. That trust has been built over many years and has earned loyalty from agents and clients alike.

- **What are the biggest changes to your brokerage you have on the books for 2019? Why?**

  Our fully integrated backend platform, which brings together all of our vendors into one place. It includes the CRM Contactually, reputation management tool Lumentus, automated digital advertising tool Adwerx and digital open house app Spacio. We are excited to invest in our proprietary technology in this way and stay on the cutting edge, and cannot wait to introduce it to our agents.

- **What keeps you up at night as a brokerage leader?**

  Always looking forward to what is next when it comes to technology. I am also concerned about competitors with near bottomless pockets. We must ensure agents recognize the unique value we offer, and continuously update our value proposition to meet modern consumer demands.

  We have been successful, and I would rather be paranoid than not. This motivates me – the competition raises my adrenaline. I like where we are. With its significant worldwide reach, the Sotheby's International Realty brand is a big asset.

- **How are you outperforming newer brokerage business models?**

  We have been effectively innovating since we launched in 1949. Other firms are introducing their own tech platforms, but they have not been selling real estate for decades. Part of success is growth, but a more important part is execution, and we have proved the ability to execute profitably over decades. Talking is different than executing.

  We have a long-standing reputation for providing exceptional services and support. Real estate is a relationship business not a product business. Technology is great and an important complement, but it will never replace the relationships that connect agents and consumers.

- **Where do you think newer models have an edge? What are you doing about them?**

  Not having to be profitable in the short term because up-front funding gives some of these newer models an edge. They have also been good at including technology in their salesmanship. Yet, when you realize that much of this technology is provided by vendors accessible to all brokers, you understand that a lot of that promised edge is just marketing and story.

  We are working to address this. Our own technology is singular and award-winning, and we are working to communicate that better. We are also focusing on communication that highlights the trust and culture our firm cultivates.

- **What do you see as the biggest long-term threat to your business?**

  We as brokerages are the primary interface at the beginning of the real estate transaction. But we are seeing organizations like Zillow Group, for example, becoming a larger and larger presence at the top of the real estate sales funnel. That is something brokers should be watching closely. Zillow Group relies on our listings, so the horse has not left the barn in that relationship. The vast majority of deals are still done through local MLSs throughout the US.

  Another threat is the industry's imbalanced capitalistic environment, with some new companies not needing to make money in the short term.

- **Do you think the residential real estate brokerage business is at a significant crossroad?**

  It has been at a crossroad. With technology changing the old style of doing business and improving the consumer experience, the old way does not work anymore. If you do not start with technology to help the consumer, your value proposition is eroding.

  Agents need real-time information to be the experts consumers increasingly demand. Business will increasingly be driven by relationships and high levels of service.

- **What do you think will be your firm's biggest differentiator in 2020?**

  The Sotheby's International Realty network will continue to deliver the most sophisticated marketing and exposure. As we reposition our branding and public relations to emphasize our quality technology, we feel we will stand out through our association with the Sotheby's International Realty brand, long-standing relationships and great technology.

Breunich heads of one of the world's largest Sotheby's International Realty affiliates in William Pitt-Julia B. Fee Sotheby's International Realty. The firm's over 1,000 agents in twenty seven offices in Connecticut, Massachusetts and New York do $4.2 billion in annual sales.

04 Understanding The Housing Supply Crisis

Why Rising Inventory Levels Will Likely Remain Low

The US is in the longest housing shortage in the modern era, and brokers and agents are feeling its impact. Despite a thriving economy and intense buyer demand, sales are lagging, buyers cannot find affordable homes and potential sellers are staying put because few to no homes are available should they sell. Even signs of a cooling market cropping up across the country, real estate brokerages and their agents recognize the significant, persistent housing shortage holding back a flourishing real estate market.

In this chapter, T3 Sixty presents the forces shaping real estate's low inventory and the levers that the industry, government and others need to pull to alleviate the current record low inventory holding housing back.

Choking Inventory

> "Inventory is defined by three key stats: the number of homes available on the market, months of supply and the average number of days listings stay on market."

Low inventory and rising home prices stifle many first-time homebuyers' homeownership dreams, but cautious homebuilders, tight credit and a glut of investor-owned single-family homes play a role, too. The previous period of extended low inventory — in the early nineties — was less intense than the current housing shortage, primarily due to higher demand from a larger population.

That sounds bleak, but while signals point to this inventory shortage stretching for another decade, trends suggest the housing market will eventually return to normal. Indeed, many markets are seeing years-long feverish demand begin to cool as 2018 draws to a close. A normal market is defined by a balance between buyer and seller demand and a return of homeownership rates to historical averages.

In August 2018, NAR projections for full-year 2018 existing-home sales stood at 5.3 million and new-home sales at 631,000, which is approximately 700,000 units and 400,000 units below the norm, respectively. With a healthy, growing economy, tight inventory is the biggest factor dragging home sales down: demand is there, but homes are not.

> "For 2018, 6 million existing home sales and 1 million new home sales should be the normal run rate. That represents a 14 percent boost in overall home sales from projected 2018 levels."

Inventory levels have fallen for three straight years and for eight of the past ten. From twelve months of supply at the depth of the downturn in mid-2010, in August 2018 it would only take 4.3 months to exhaust total inventory at the current sales pace. According to NAR, a balanced market is six to seven months of inventory.

Moreover, buyers scoop up homes that do hit the market at an incredibly swift pace, with the average days on market hovering at approximately twenty-six days in mid-2018, the fewest since NAR began tracking the stat in 2011. Starter homes in many markets across the country experience bidding wars. This has been years in the making.

As the real estate market began to recover from the Great Recession, homes started flying off the shelves and homebuilders, burned by the recession years, did not keep up with buyer demand. This period of exceptionally low inventory began in 2013.

Low Inventory by the Numbers

Existing-home sales, which comprise more than 90 percent of all homes sold, have struggled to inch higher in 2018. They dipped 2.2 percent in the first half of 2018 from the same period a year previous. Given the country's positive economic backdrop, this should not be happening.

Several key numbers highlight the country's extreme housing shortage. According to the Current Population Survey by the U.S. Census Bureau and the U.S. Bureau of Labor Statistics, the US population rises by a net of approximately 2 to 3 million people each year from immigration and births. This rise leads to approximately 1.1 to 1.3 million new

Low Inventory Numbers

Inventory is defined by three key stats: the number of homes available on the market, months of supply (how long it would take to exhaust supply given current demand) and, an indirect indicator, the average number of days listings stay on market. September 2018 numbers indicate the market still suffers from extremely low inventory, though the average days homes stay on the market is rising.

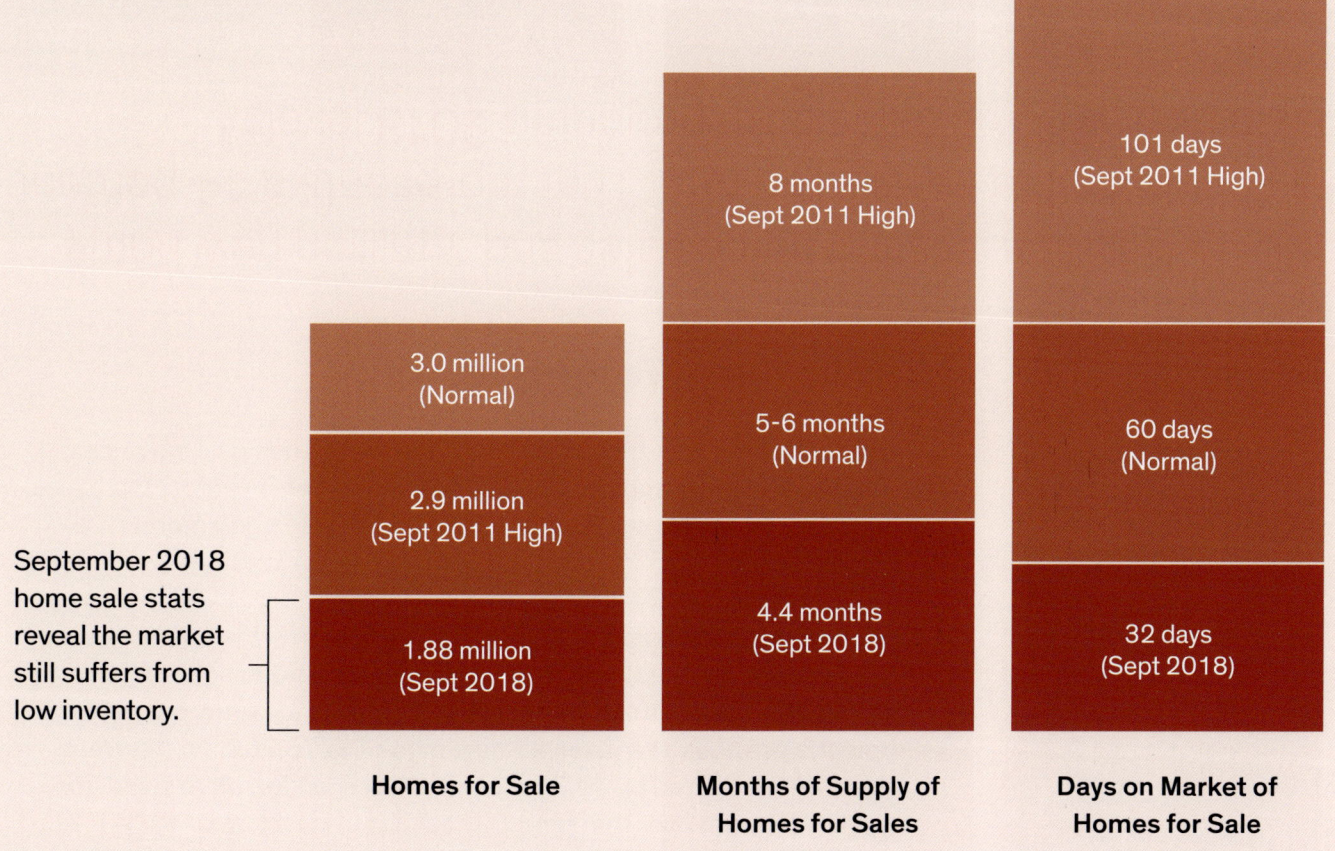

September 2018 home sale stats reveal the market still suffers from low inventory.

Source: National Association of Realtors

household formations and corresponding new housing demands each year.

Approximately 300,000 to 500,000 housing units get demolished or become uninhabitable each year, a number equal to less than half of 1 percent of total housing units.

Combining new household formation and demolished units, midpoint estimates suggest that the market needs 1.6 million new homes each year just to keep up with population growth. Naturally, demand wanes during penny-pinching recession years and increases during healthy economic times.

Inventory is defined by three key stats: the number of homes available on the market, months of supply (how long it would take to exhaust supply given current demand) and, an indirect indicator, the average number of days listings stay on market.

In June 2018, there were 1.95 million homes on the market, 4.3 months of supply and an average days on market of 26 days. According to NAR estimates during a nomal inventory period, these numbers would be three million homes for sale, five to six months of supply and an average days on market of approximately sixty days.

Home Price, Wage Imbalance

The pattern is clear: Low inventory leads to fast-rising home prices, which then deters homebuyers. Conversely, when inventory increases, home prices should moderate, which then should bring more homebuyers.

Because of the housing shortage, home price growth continues to exceed wage increases, which always produces a housing problem over time. In June 2018, the national median home price grew 5.2 percent from the previous year to an all-time high of $276,900. (In the West, home prices soared by 10.3 percent). Wages, on the other hand, rose only 2.7 percent over that time.

> "Combining new household formation and demolished units, midpoint estimates suggest that the market needs 1.6 million new homes each year just to keep up with population growth."

California has a particularly acute housing shortage. The price of a typical home in the Golden State rose by 67 percent in the past six years; while income grew by only 15 percent, a huge imbalance. These accumulated imbalances simply cannot last. NAR expects many markets, such as California and Colorado, to start contracting. In short, low inventory has pushed prices unsustainably high.

New Home Sales

Over the past decade, builders added just under 9 million new homes, compared to the 16 million homes that would be considered normal — the market has a cumulative shortage of over 7 million homes. After accounting for the need to pull back after overproduction during the housing bubble years, the current shortfall likely stands a bit lower, approximately 5 million units.

In 2018, housing starts may hit 1.3 million, short of the annual historical average of approximately 1.5 million as calculated by NAR. Note that the 2018 figure marks the best in a decade, which underscores just how much the construction industry has lagged in recent years. From 2009, when the Great Recession was deepening, to today, housing starts averaged just 885,000 per year. That is just half of the historic annual average.

The building industry does not have the resources to produce 5 million new homes in a year. Therefore, it could take at least three additional years, into 2021, for the industry to fully recover from such a severe shortfall. If builders build, buyers will buy.

Although, new homes have higher price tags than existing-homes — with August 2018 median prices of $320,000 for a new home and $265,000 for an existing-home — new homes are showing sales gains, while existing-homes remain closer to neutral. Homebuilders sit in a great position today — they can usually quickly sell what they build.

According to NAR, new-home sales should rise approximately 10 percent in 2019, even with higher interest rates because of the accumulated pent-up demand for housing that the existing-home market cannot fully satisfy. Only an economic recession and massive job cuts could undercut this new-home sales forecast.

A new normal?

Young adults remain single for longer periods and have their first child later in life. Given that marriages and childbirths serve as big

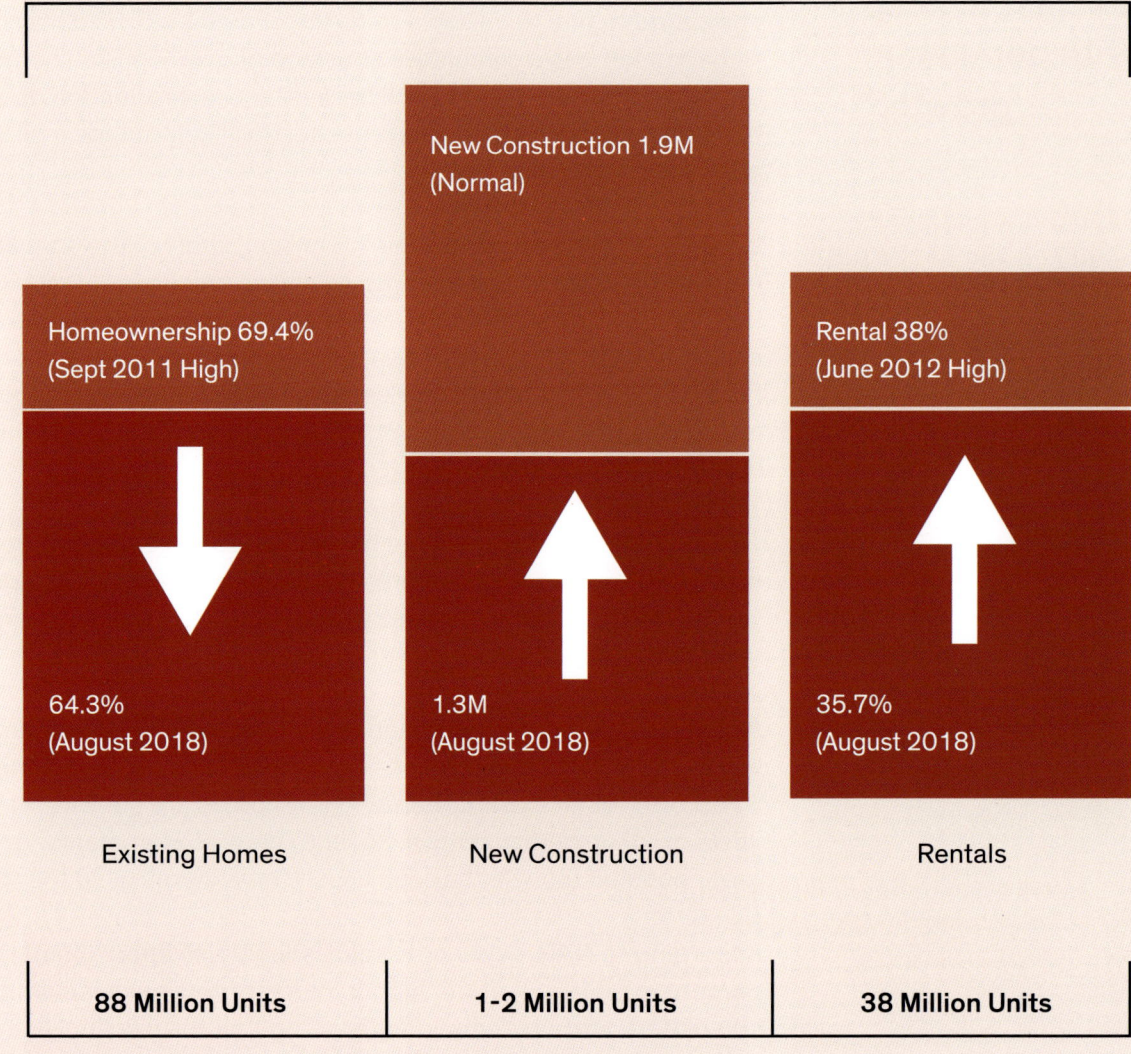

homebuying triggers, the industry may have to reexamine traditional homebuying trends and accept a new normal.

While this demographic trend may suggest less demand for new homes, the opposite may actually be true. Historically, larger families occupied just one housing unit. Today, fewer married couples and more single people could mean a higher number of households and a corresponding increased need for housing. Both scenarios are plausible — time will tell how these trends play out.

Investor-Owned Homes

Investors jumped in to buy single-family houses during the Great Recession and turned them into rentals. Roughly speaking, investors own 5 million more single-family homes than they typically would. When supply and demand even out in the coming years, investors will begin to sell, adding another important inventory stream as housing rebalances.

Mixed Signals

Existing-home sales dropped in the first half of 2018 compared to the prior year. However, new home sales climbed by 7 percent with homebuilders expressing continued optimism about market conditions.

Consumers, meanwhile, have less optimism, with 39 percent strongly indicating they feel it was a good time to buy in the second quarter 2018 compared to 43 percent the year prior, according to NAR's second quarter 2018 Housing Opportunities and Market Experience consumer survey.

Mortgage rates have reached decade-highs yet have not dampened home prices, which have surged to all-time highs.

These conflicting signals highlight the highly complex housing market. Regardless, brokers and agents across the country know, as do their clients, that low inventory has driven the market for years. It appears it will continue do so for the foreseeable future.

Rising interest rates and rising home prices typically do not occur together, but a persistent underproduction of new homes over the last decade has created this low-inventory scenario. One thing is clear: Builders need to ramp up production to alleviate the building pressure from low inventory. New home construction is the one low-inventory relief valve.

> "Because of the housing shortage, home price growth continues to exceed wage increases, which always produces a housing problem over time."

Why Housing Supply is Critical for a Healthy Society

In the second quarter 2018, there were 77.9 million owner-occupied units and 43.3 million were renter-occupied, for a homeownership rate of 64.2 percent. A rate of 66 percent is considered normal for the US. Although a two percent difference may seem small, it still represents millions of households. At just over 35 percent, the rate is particularly low among young adults under age 35, the lowest rate for that group in the last three decades.

This has repercussions beyond fewer commission checks for real estate brokerages and agents – lower homeownership rates have deeper societal repercussions. The prolonged extreme low inventory makes the American Dream of homeownership harder to attain for more people. The feeling of out-of-reach homeownership takes a psychological toll and increases societal stress.

Along with higher wealth accumulation, homeowners show better overall adjustment than renters. Studies show that homeownership contributes to better test scores for children, less socially deviant behavior such as juvenile delinquency and overall better health.

Economic Backdrop

By many measures, the economy has outperformed expectations. The stimulus from massive tax cuts and business deregulation has boosted both consumer and business spending. For 2018, the US Gross Domestic Product (GDP) growth rate – often used to assess the health of a country's overall economy — looks to exceed 3 percent for the first time since 2005.

This solid growth rate, however, does not come without associated costs. The pumped-up spending could fizzle out. Even if sustainable, the annual budget deficit has increased substantially and the national debt is approaching the critical point of 100 percent GDP.

The US government's extra borrowing has contributed to rising interest rates. Given that interest rate changes greatly affect the housing market, logic suggests rising rates should dampen demand. The flourishing economy has kept demand high, however.

For example, the economy has over 18 million net new jobs since the depths of the Great Recession in 2010, and the unemployment rate has plunged below 4 percent in 2018. *Help Wanted* signs are everywhere and job openings exceed the number of those unemployed seeking work at times.

Rising wages indicate that companies are desperately trying to hold on to existing workers. Filings for jobless benefits by recently fired employees were at historic lows in mid-2018. After the cuts to the corporate tax rates in late 2017, companies can easily afford to pay higher salaries as corporate profits have soared.

Furthermore, the country's aggregate wealth surpassed the $100 trillion mark for the first time in early 2018 as home prices and stock prices set new highs. For comparison, the nation's pre-Recession total wealth stood at $67 trillion in 2007 before sliding to $55 trillion during the 2009 depths. With so much wealth and so many jobs, should not home sales be heading higher?

Economic Headwinds

Tax reform has played a role in dampening home sales. While real estate agents have expressed concern about the potential elimination of mortgage interest and property tax deductions, the tax bill passed with a sizable mortgage interest deduction allowance (up to $750,000 in newly originated mortgages and a $1 million for existing mortgages).

> " ... the country's aggregate wealth surpassed the $100 trillion mark for the first time ... "

Property tax often accounts for the biggest portion of overall state and local taxes, but homeowners can deduct up to $10,000 of these.

NAR's calculations show that over 90 percent of homeowners and homebuyers could fully deduct both mortgage interest and property tax if they wanted to. Even in high tax states such as Connecticut, over 70 percent of homeowners could fully deduct mortgage interest and property taxes.

However, far fewer households will itemize their tax returns as the number of filers using simpler and larger standard deductions will grow. In other words, tax breaks have become a less compelling incentive to buy a home than in the past. More Americans receive a tax break whether they buy a home or stay a renter.

How To Lift Inventory

Low inventory has had an outsized influence on the real estate market in recent years and will likely continue to do so, at least in the near future. Several key factors can bring more housing on the market including lowering construction costs, easing the permitting process, revising restrictive condo laws and incentivizing residents to support local construction.

Ensure Manageable Home Construction Costs

Rising homebuilding material costs slow builders. The lumber tariff the Trump Administration pushed for harms the industry. It limits job creation associated with more homebuilding, raises prices for American consumers and keeps homeownership rates from rising in an expanding economy.

Although analysts could debate the pros and cons of the Dodd-Frank financial regulations for large and systemically important banks, such as Bank of America and Goldman Sachs, they unambiguously harmed small-sized banks. But legislators are undoing part of that legislation.

Before the housing crash, community banks were the primary source of construction loans for small-sized homebuilders. However, the new financial rules hampered community banks from making those loans. As a consequence, big national and regional homebuilders got larger, while smaller homebuilders struggled to get loans.

With relaxed rules for small banks, small homebuilder activity should pick up. Before the Recession, small homebuilders built more new homes in total than all the publicly listed homebuilders combined. More builders should benefit consumers, as competition will dampen builder profit margins and lower home costs.

Construction Labor
Homebuilders do not only face challenges with high costs of aluminum, steel and lumber. High construction labor costs play a role in slowing their momentum, too.

While construction wages are, on average, rising faster than other industries, a deepening labor shortage and a consequent massive jump in wages will hinder homebuilders going forward. Increasing the supply of qualified construction labor will spur homebuilding, but few skilled workers exist.

Communities can alleviate the labor shortage by placing more emphasis on vocational training: carpentry, plumbing, and electrical trades for students not as academically inclined as their peers. Not everyone should attend college and bear the cost of student debt.

A special state-run program in Tennessee offers free vocational training to laid-off workers who meet a set of specified criteria. The program ensures that unemployed workers receive immediate training for in-demand skills such as those related to construction. Other states could explore similar programs.

Because of exceptionally low unemployment rates and the difficulty of finding skilled labor, South Dakota and Iowa have resorted to novel methods. These states use nonviolent prisoners to fill the void of construction labor. Paying willing workers a good wage to learn desirable skills, while they help solve the housing crisis is a win-win. Inmates leave prison with valuable work skills and savings, which can deter a return to crime.

Some may not like the idea of employing prisoners for construction work, but it offers one straightforward solution to the labor shortage. Training more construction workers from a variety of sources would boost homebuilding, increase housing supply and bring more homes to market at prices more households can afford.

Other solutions include spurring able adults not in the workforce to jump into construction jobs. While the unemployment rate is at a historic low, the employment rate of all adults remains low. Before the Recession, 64 percent of adults had jobs; now only 60.4 percent do. Analysts consider adults who do not have a job and do not search for one as out of the labor force, not unemployed.

> "Increasing the supply of qualified construction labor will spur homebuilding."

In the future, factories will produce and ship out more complete components of new homes. Builders will then assemble the pieces onsite. Automation and accompanying productivity improvements will increase over time. Nevertheless, builders will still need skilled construction laborers at worksites to assure a steady flow of new homes meet demand and the growing population.

Streamline New-Home Permitting

Local communities can also improve housing supply by eliminating overly stringent permitting processes and high impact fees. For example, some localities in California require over $100,000 in impact fees before a shovel can turn the soil on a new home site.

No wonder, then, that the San Francisco Bay Area saw only 14,000 single-family new homes built in the past three years despite a robust 183,000 net new jobs in the same period. The Atlanta metro market experienced a similar number of new jobs yet saw 72,000 new single-family homes. That explains Atlanta faces less of an affordability crisis then San Francisco-Oakland market.

> "The future of autonomous vehicles and increased use of ride-sharing services, will permit more building with less parking space."

Revise Condo-Development/Management Laws

Local communities should consider making it easier for developers, or even encourage them, to repurpose declining commercial buildings – such as empty shopping malls or older, dilapidated properties – into residential condominium units.

Localities can also promote compact development patterns in land-restricted regions. If unable to spread out over a large area, builders can build up vertically. The future of autonomous vehicles and increased use of ride-sharing services, such as Uber and Lyft, will permit more building with less parking space.

Reworking the detrimental condominium defect laws would also help spur condo development. In Denver, for example, condominium owners can bring a class-action lawsuit against a builder if dissatisfied with their condo's construction; all it takes is one, in fact. Builders must then compensate all the condominium owners, not just those who waged a complaint.

No surprise then that while apartment construction boomed in Denver, condominiums have not. Communities should consider updating their condominium defect laws to support homebuilding and increased housing inventory.

Incentive Residents Around New Construction

Localities or the state should consider turning NIMBYism (Not in My Backyard) into YIMBYism (Yes in My Backyard) by providing financial incentives to neighbors affected by new developments such as a one-year property tax relief. Although this lowers tax revenue, the temporary tax break incentivizes current residents to get on board with the inconvenience that homebuilding can cause. The town wins in the long run as more tax revenue will fill its coffers when residents move into the new housing units.

What Brokers Can Do

Brokers can help increase inventory by supporting their local Realtor association in advocating for local homebuilding. Some local measures that can increase inventory include relaxing stringent zoning laws, lowering impact fees and providing construction-related vocational training.

Brokers can monitor their local inventory trends by checking monthly data on housing permits issued locally and share that knowledge with agents and consumers. If permitting lags behind jobs, then brokers

> "Rising interest rates and rising home prices typically do not occur together, but a persistent underproduction of new homes over the last decade has created this low-inventory scenario."

know demand will increase; if vice-versa, they know demand will shrink. In a balanced market, one new housing permit is typically issued for every net 1.5 new jobs.

Forecast

How the market plays out in the upcoming years depends on how many of the factors above play out. But if current trends hold, inventory should slowly tick up.

When more homes do hit the market, the growth of home prices will slow and more homes will become reasonably affordable for a larger portion of middle-income households. In this case, an increase in jobs will immediately lead to an increase in home sales. As housing inventory slowly increases, homebuyer psychology will play a role in the housing market's track to normal.

For example, some homesellers waiting for higher prices will suddenly find that area homes sit on the market for longer as area buyers perceive available homes as overpriced. Other sellers will jump into the market, wanting to cash out at what they perceive as a market peak. Inventory will build quickly. Some buyers will wonder if prices may drop and wait a bit, not only to get a better deal but also because no one wants to be stuck with a depreciating asset.

Buyers then will swing back and decide to make offers because the economy is good, they can now afford to and they recognize the long-term financial benefit of owning a home. As buyers come back, prices stabilize and begin to rise in a more moderate fashion. So, as inventory rises, a short-lived market chaos could ensue before things level out.

What to Watch

Rising Interest Rates
One big external risk to this forecast is the speed at which interest rates rise. The market can absorb moderate changes. The above forecast is based on mortgage rates moving up to 5 percent by mid-2019 and not surpassing 6 percent until 2020.

Although these rates are higher than the sub-4 percent rates of recent years, job creation and higher inventory will keep affordability near their historically normal range. Recall that mortgage rates averaged 8 percent in 2000 and everyone cheered when they fell to 6 percent by the end of 2002. The industry is just getting back to the 6 percent mortgage rate range. If interest rates rise more sharply, then worrying becomes justified.

On the other hand, interest rates could decline, though this will unlikely occur for a prolonged period. Or the stock market could correct or the economy measurably slow.

Inflation

Other factors could drive rates up. Broad consumer prices have risen again and have recently jumped above the desired 2 percent rate. High inflation will force lenders to charge higher interest rates to compensate for the inflation-driven loss in purchasing power of returned money. As the national debt continues to rise, the government must issue more bonds. Since the Federal Reserve will not buy those bonds, as it did in the last housing market downturn under Quantitative Easing, the government will have to offer higher interest rates attract bond buyers.

Takeaway

Low inventory has stymied real estate brokers and agents and their clients for years and trends suggests it will continue to do so for the foreseeable future. The industry is in the middle of the longest housing shortage in the modern era.

Toward the end of 2018, some markets began to see movement to increased inventory, marked by longer days on market and dampening price increases. The good news is that this inventory uptick should improve as homebuilding ticks up, home price appreciation moderates and a more balanced market returns. The bad news is that this could take a decade, and could take longer if interest rates shoot up higher than expected or new legislation hampers credit for homebuilders or consumers.

Brokerages and agents should monitor their local markets closely to educate their clients. They can also choose to advocate for local homebuilding-friendly policies as new construction will play the central role in alleviating the industry's low inventory.

Lead Contributor:

Lawrence Yun
Lawrence is Chief Economist and Senior Vice President of Research at the National Association of Realtors. He oversees, and is responsible for, a wide range of research activity for the association including NAR's Existing Home Sales statistics, Affordability Index, and Home Buyers and Sellers Profile Report. Lawrence can be reached at lyun@realtors.org.

Chris Raveis, President of Sales, William Raveis Real Estate and Affiliates

From the Frontlines

What are the chief industry changes that affect your brokerage today?

Technology continues to advance at a rapid-pace, making the real estate process much more efficient, while also making agents more valuable throughout the transaction cycle. When the market gets hot, as it has been for the last several years, we see new models pop up. When the market hits a downturn, they dry up. We monitor the elements of these models that consumers like and integrate those components into our business model.

- **What are you doing about those changes?**

In 2015, we decided to completely overhaul our technology. We had our previous technology for eight years, which was cutting edge when we first rolled it out. It was time for us to reevaluate and develop a platform that again would be unique and top-of-the-line. We decided to invest heavily and pull the trigger.

We spent two years selecting the best vendors we could find. We included our top agents in various markets across our footprint in the process.

We now have a customized and proprietary single-sign-on platform built on a Microsoft Office 365 base that centralizes all our technology for agents in one place. All our vendors integrate with each other through APIs, so it is seamless to use on mobile. Our tech platform includes the Moxi Works CRM and CMA, Microsoft Office, Microsoft email and digital transaction management platform SkySlope.

We know what it is like to build and program our own technology – we did it during the last housing boom, in the early 2000s. We had a real estate tech company, Home-Link, which provided software and integration consulting to 300 brokerages across the US. This time we decided to focus on real estate rather than building technology. Whether building the technology ourselves or using other vendors, we know that, in addition to a good tech system, implementation and training really drives tech results.

- **What keeps you up at night as a brokerage leader?**

It is always about people, about talent, about ensuring that we have great talent leading the company. We are always hyperfocused on developing this talent and supporting a high-functioning management team.

- **How are you outperforming newer brokerage business models?**

The process of starting something new, gaining traction and driving initial growth does not necessarily translate into operating a profitable long-term business built on constantly reinforcing and proving its value. That is where we stand out from the newer models. Agents know we are here to support them – we have proved that for over forty-five years.

There are no silver bullets; it takes hard work, and they have seen us work. We have credibility. We know how to grow a business. We have done this and we help our agents do it, too.

The culture we have built over a long period of time sets us apart. We are also a family business, a rare occurrence in our industry and something that newer models do not have. We treat our company as a family. Our agents and staff have access to the owners and leadership. We get to know our people. We are all attached to what we do and we rally around a common vision. We are a family business to everyone in our company.

We have a high-service model, which is different from many tech-based newer models. We provide a lot of services and value to agents – centered on helping them grow their business. We offer a full-service technology platform, a branding program, coaching and mentoring and, overall, serve as proactive partners in their business. Our consumers receive comprehensive service and an agent empowered to provide great value in all phases of the homeselling and homebuying journey.

- **Where do you think newer models have an edge? What are you doing about them?**

    They do not have to make money. They can burn through a lot of cash before figuring out where they land. That is their challenge. Running a business is easy if you have a lot to spend and do not have to worry about making a profit. The hard part is operating a business and maintaining sustainable margins.

Some newer venture-backed companies are making noise in a couple of our markets. Bottom line, you cannot build a strong culture without working at it for years, consistently proving everyday who you are as a company.

New models try to build perceived culture by spending a lot of money on strong public relations and ad campaigns. At the end of the day, you cannot buy culture, you must earn it. That is where the hard work lies.

We have a strong business model and we are close to our people. We know some people will leave and others will join us, that has always been the case. But one thing holds true, we have been here for forty-five years, we have innovated and grown every year, and we only get stronger as we evolve.

- **What do you think will be your firm's biggest differentiator in 2020?**

    Culture sets us apart as does our business that helps agents grow their businesses by supporting them with the best resources, our experience and a tremendous amount of hands-on training.

Chris Raveis, along with his brother Ryan, runs William Raveis Real Estate Inc. as co-president. Their father William Raveis founded the company in 1974. Chris oversees the brokerage's 4,000 agents and 130 branches and his brother Ryan manages headquarter operations and the company divisions that support its offices. The firm's footprint includes New York, Connecticut, Rhode Island, Massachusetts, Vermont, New Hampshire, Maine and Florida. In 2018, it ranked as the nation's twelfth largest brokerage by annual sales volume.

03 The Brokerage Technology Conundrum

How To Develop a Smart Tech Strategy

All brokers know technology is rapidly reshaping the residential real estate brokerage industry. That knowledge, however, does not necessarily drive intelligent, productive action, as technology does not fall in many brokers' wheelhouse. But it should. Integrated broker platforms, easy-to-use marketing systems and agent tools, and APIs that seamlessly connect disparate systems increase the power and advantage of tech-savvy brokerages with smarter, more automated, more integrated, more mobile, faster tools every day. These systems create efficiencies and insights that will increasingly separate the brokerages who leverage them from those who do not.

This chapter provides a framework for all brokerages to begin building (or continue to build) a smart, sustaining technology strategy.

The Brokerage Technology Landscape

> "Technology — its the one thing that has seeped in everywhere. How frightfully delightful."
>
> Stefan Swanepoel

Many traditional brokerages are grappling with implementing technology into businesses built in a pre-digital era, while newer, tech-age brokerages are finding scale and rising fast. Regardless of how or when brokerages implement technology, success will increasingly depend on how much and what technology they bring on, the strategy that guides the effort and how well the tools integrate.

The residential real estate brokerage technology landscape can be intimidating and overwhelming. The staggering number of tools, the fierce independence of agents, the velocity of constant change and the exploding number of tech vendors all make smart technology decisions a significant broker challenge.

That is why folding technology decisions into a clear strategy is critically important. Without a clear outline, it is impossible to benchmark results, get companywide buy-in or even hope to implement tools at the adoption rates necessary to make the technology financially and operationally viable.

To help brokerages build sound strategies, T3 Sixty has mapped the residential real estate brokerage industry technology landscape. We have identified seventy-eight distinct tech categories related to the consumer's homebuying journey. Brokerage companies must consider most, if not all, of these categories when designing a comprehensive, smart technology strategy.

Similar tech landscape funnels exist for agent retention and recruiting, but this chapter focuses on tech related to the consumer funnel as it is the most prominent and important.

The Real Estate Brokerage Consumer Funnel

One thing should be made clear before diving in: There is no all-in-one brokerage technology solution. Different parts of the customer journey require expertise and specialized systems beyond the scope of a single technology vendor.

The brokerage consumer funnel has four sections; each relates to a specific stage of the consumer journey, ranging from initial contact to past client. It follows the traditional marketing funnel.

Brokerage Consumer Sales Funnel

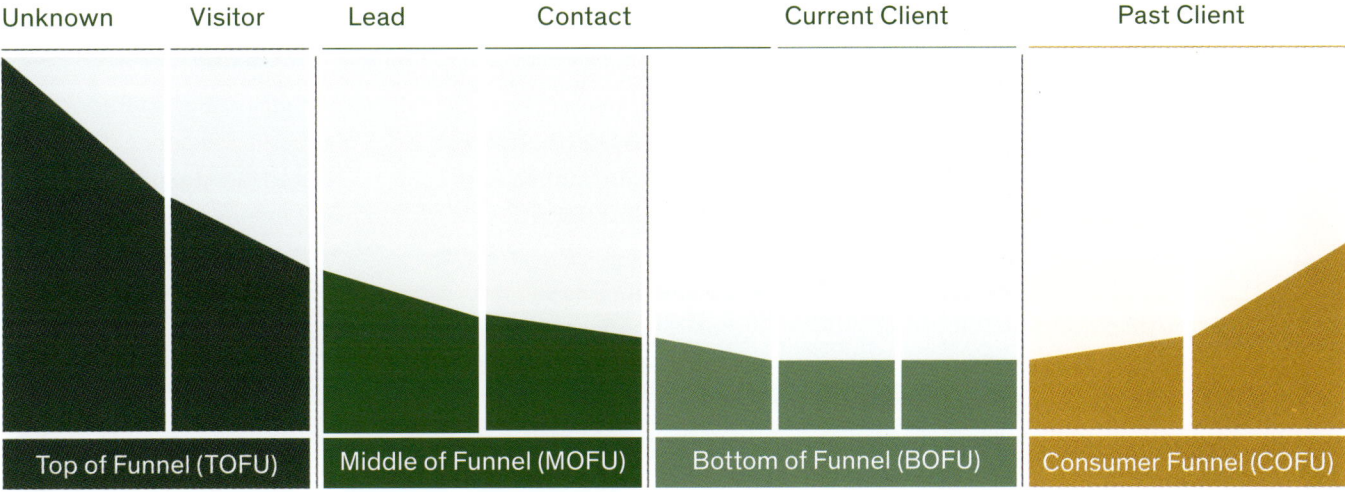

Source: T3 Sixty

The journey starts at the top of the sales funnel (TOFU) with brand awareness marked by a consumer visiting a website or seeing an ad. It continues in the middle of the funnel (MOFU) with initial engagement, when consumers opt in to an email list, sign up for a listing search or contact an agent for more information. At the bottom of the funnel (BOFU), consumers become a buyer or seller client. On the customer side of the funnel (COFU), clients become past customers, leave reviews for brokerages and agents. Brokerages and agents stay in touch with these customers and maintain relationships, often with the help of CRMs.

Real Estate Brokerage Tech Landscape

Based on the consumer tech landscape developed by T3 Sixty, brokerage companies have seventy-eight tech categories to consider related to the consumer journey.

Each category represents a distinct technology that brokerages can make a financial or strategic decision on. For example, whether and how to do search engine marketing makes up one of the tech decisions a brokerage can make. Others include whether and how to do Facebook marketing, video marketing, advertising with realtor.com and Zillow, website remarketing, etc.

All tech categories are presented in the consumer tech landscape on the following page.

Consumer Technology Landscape

Top of Funnel (TOFU)

- Search Engine Marketing
- Search Engine Optimization
- Facebook Advertising System
- Zillow Group, Realtor.com, etc.
- Predictive Marketing
- Just Listed/Just Sold/Farming
- Video/Display Advertising
- Digital Sphere Marketing
- Social Media Management System
- Social Content Strategy
- Company Website

- IDX Property Search
- Website Lead Gen Platform
- Mobile Website/Mobile App
- Agent Websites/Blog
- YouTube/Vimeo/Wistia/Other
- Virtual and 3D Tours
- School/Neighborhood Pages
- Lifestyle/Content Data
- Relocation Guide
- Drive Time
- AVM/Home Price Estimate

- Housing Market Reports
- Lead Intelligence/Big Data
- Lead Management System
- Sign Rider Lead Capture Solution
- Open House Lead Capture
- Outbound Listing Syndication
- Live Chat

Middle of Funnel (MOFU)

- Customer Management (CRM)
- Marketing Center (Print/Digital)
- Market/Home Value Report
- Showing Solution
- Listing Alerts
- Reverse Prospecting

- Comparative Market Analysis
- Listing Presentation
- Coming Soon Database
- Private Inventory Database
- Texting Platform
- Video Email and Messaging

- AI Virtual Assistant
- Sales Pipeline Reporting
- Email Marketing
- Lead Routing System
- Dialer

Bottom of Funnel (BOFU)

- Forms Solution
- E-Signature
- Transaction Management

- Seller Reports
- Relocation/Referral Management
- Accounting System

- General Ledger
- Commission Calculation System
- Broker Performance Dashboard

Consumer Funnel (COFU)

- Testimonial/Ratings Platform
- Review Sites (Google, Yelp, etc.)
- Industry Reviews (Zillow, realtor.com)

- Repeat/Referral Marketing
- Repeat/Referral Intelligence
- Intranet/Single-Sign-On Hub
- Email, Contacts & Calendar

- Document Management/Sharing
- Agent Roster Management
- Recruiting Platform/CRM

Source: T3 Sixty

A well-thought-out strategy includes an analysis of each category. Brokerages do not need activity in each category, but should strategically decide which to employ and which to skip and why. Given its broad scope, brokerage technology is necessarily an exercise in priorities.

As noted above, this chart just addresses technology related to the consumer journey. Brokerages should perform similar exercises related to agent recruiting and retention and hardware.

Technology Improves Brokerage Operations

Technology touches every facet of a real estate brokerage. Diving into specific tech categories reveals just how powerful and useful technology can be in streamlining brokerage operations. Three categories are presented below to illustrate this.

Company Website

Real estate brokerages with sophisticated websites that support their lead generation strategies and tie into their CRMs realize significant efficiencies. For one, a fast, well-designed website presents a strong brand to consumers and agents, starting relationships out on the right foot.

A good initial impression is just the tip of the iceberg. Sophisticated websites can align perfectly with marketing campaigns to increase conversion rates. They can also automate lead distribution to agents and track user behavior, which increases the quality and speed of lead responses.

Powerful websites also support detailed measurement, which allows brokerages to refine content strategies, calls to action and more to up engagement and conversion rates.

Some brokerages supply these sophisticated websites to their agents, which aids retention and recruitment. Maintaining a good website is difficult, and agents appreciate when their broker can help them with this key technology. A good website will also increase their productivity, which, for brokerages who share their agents' commissions, raises all boats.

Transaction Management

Digital transaction management platforms such as dotloop (dotloop.com), SkySlope (skyslope.com) and DocuSign (docusign.com) give brokerages and their agents an all-digital, mobile way to start, complete and track their transactions. These platforms integrate with other tools to eliminate duplicate entry, which streamlines work and decreases errors.

These systems, with e-signatures and full-featured mobile applications, can also automate some portions of the transaction, in addition to providing compliance review and 24/7 cloud access to documents and contracts. Brokers, staff and agents no longer need to go the office to review a paper document — they can do it wherever they are, at their convenience.

This speeds up the transaction process, saving real estate offices time and money and improves consumer experience.

These systems' reporting features also give brokerages real-time data on every aspect of company transaction performance, from companywide metrics, to office- and agent-specific reporting. These can be used to optimize forecasting, coaching and more.

These systems often replace brokers' need to use and store paper documents. This eliminates staff time and storage costs associated

> "Technology is fundamentally reengineering the entire real estate brokerage industry."

with managing paper. Support personnel no longer need to review physical sheets of paper from each office, which supports centralization efforts. Brokerages can also keep tighter control of their compliance processes on these systems, forcing proper handling of all documents before parties move to the next step.

Digital transaction management has transformed the economics and margins for many brokerages, giving them speed, accountability and automated features that make them and their agents more efficient. With new automation features powered by artificial intelligence that eliminate rote brokerage staff and agent tasks, these platforms are also getting more powerful.

Transaction management is one of the most popular categories brokerages address.

CRMs

Powerful CRMs are a real estate game-changer. Brokerages who supply them to agents, increase loyalty and increase lead conversion rates. The most sophisticated CRMs automate contact information, record and document contact events, use artificial intelligence, big data and behavioral analytics to pinpoint contacts who may be likely to transact soon, and offer sophisticated followup options through email, social media and more.

In many ways, good CRMs optimize agents' operations. It becomes their hub — the lifeblood of their business, where they measure, track and cultivate relationships. The insights and tools they provide increase efficiency, up conversion rates and ensure less business falls through the cracks.

For more on CRMs, see the *2018 Swanepoel Trends Report* chapter, Trend No. 8, "Smart CRMs Go Mainstream."

Getting Tech Up to Speed

If brokerages recognize they have tech holes or feel the need to get started, now is the time to push the pedal. As new brokerage business models grow with smart, integrated tech, and traditional models rapidly integrate it, non-tech-savvy brokerages will soon not be able to compete.

Legacy brokerages, built during a much simpler technology era, have much more work to do to get up to speed. They must recognize that technology expenditures are no longer a single line item in their profit-and-loss statement, but touch every part of their company.

Brokerages should not just evaluate their own technology—using the T3 Sixty brokerage technology landscape as a guide—but also that of their competitors. Understanding competitors' tech strategies helps uncover differentiating opportunities, although a complete evaluation of all categories may be very difficult. The exercise will, however, still provide useful insights.

Modernizing a brokerage operation with technology is a daunting task. The efforts brokers put in could position their firm competitively well into the future. Success requires complete commitment, support, training, tracking and refinement.

As brokers attempt to implement a smart technology strategy, the following basic principles will help them get started: start measuring current operations, practice good operational best practices and embrace real estate's current technology reality (presented below).

Technology Landscape Worksheet

Technology	Provider	Cost	Performance	Agent Adoption	Grade 1-10	Improvement Plan
Facebook Marketing Solution	Ex. Facebook marketing provider	$1,000 per month	100,000 impressions, 1,000 clicks, 100 leads, $20 cost per lead	85%	8	Increase budget to drive more leads
CRM	Ex. CRM provider	$3,000 per month or $15 per agent per month	10,000 total email sends 1,000 contacts	40%	5	Increase marketing automation to entice more agents
Transaction Management	Ex. transaction management provider	$2,000 per month or $10 per agent per month	30 minutes processing time to close 78% of files intact	65%	7	Increase training to decrease file submission errors and processing time

Source: T3 Sixty

Refine Operations

To really leverage technology, brokerages need to implement a tech-friendly way of business — they need to be efficient, clear and measurement-focused.

That formula boils down to: Ask questions. Learn. Improve. And repeat. Brokers can find a good outline for this in Trend No. 4 in the *2018 Swanepoel Trends Report* "The Management-Empowered Brokerage Business Model."

Set the Foundation

> "Today, tech touches the entire brokerage from top to bottom."

Brokerages need to understand that this effort requires companywide buy-in — it transcends divisions and personnel. This is a fundamental reengineering of the brokerage. Before getting started, brokers must understand real estate tech's current reality. The major elements are:

- It is time to act.

- Establishing priorities and choosing which battles to fight will be a constant exercise. Determining strategic priorities are a must.

- Beware of vendors claiming they have it all. It is highly unlikely.

- There are no short cuts. This effort requires a significant investment of time, energy and money.

In developing a strategy, brokerages must determine their current technology, how much it costs and how it performs. This involves a full audit and measurement. They must also determine if agents use the technology provided to them and whether any low adoption rates are a consequence of an ineffective roll-out, support failures or the tool itself. Finally, brokerages need to uncover which technology is underperforming and why; if it is underperforming, brokerages must assess whether the cause is improper use or the technology itself.

Brokerages can use the tech landscape worksheet provided in this chapter to score their technology. They should compile the answers and review with their leadership team. The chart on page 140 is an example of how a brokerage should approach all seventy-eight categories.

After clearly outlining their current technology and determining how well they use it, brokerages should measure the performance of each technology category and identify how each contributes to their bottom line.

Making the Right Tech Choices

Next, brokerages should determine which of the seventy-eight technology categories to focus on and how. Their tech assessment will reveal underperforming tech categories, which will help them assess which to scuttle and which to improve. All technology in a brokerage's tech stack should impact at least one of the following core business areas: productivity, ROI, agent recruiting and retention and brand awareness, or marketing and advertising.

Once brokerages choose the categories they would like to focus on, they should choose how to bring the technology on. A brokerage's size, resources and model determines which ones will be the best fit. Where possible, brokerages should place priority on integrations, automation and single-sign-on to increase agent adoption and operational efficiencies. The seven brokerage tech-implementation strategies are outlined below.

Seven Implementation Strategies

Brokerages have a variety of tech-implementation strategies to choose from: build from the ground up in-house; acquire a tech company and fold into their company; make an equity investment in a tech company whose platform they intend to use; partner with a tech vendor and white-label the product; partner with best-in-class real estate tech platforms; or leverage general tech platforms not specifically built for real estate.

> "Given the breadth of a modern brokerage's tech needs, brokerages will often use a mix of these strategies to implement technology."

Given the breadth of a modern brokerage's tech needs, brokerages will often use a mix of these strategies to implement technology.

1. Build In-house

Building technology in-house requires brokerages to hire, manage, finance and operate their own tech wing. This is easier for many newer brokerages because they design technology with operations from the beginning and then organically scale it in lockstep with growth.

Building technology requires big money and significant expertise but it has advantages. Owning technology allows brokerages to focus it where and when they want, to build specific features they want in the way they want and to develop enterprise value and a competitive advantage. Keller Williams Realty, Redfin, HomeSmart, Opendoor, @properties and John L. Scott have built significant amounts of their own technology.

- ▲ **Pros.** The ability to control destiny is a big plus of this strategy. It also creates a compelling and unique competitive advantage. Brokerages can endlessly customize and tailor tools to their unique markets, brand and model.

- ▼ **Cons.** The cost to start up and maintain technology is enormous for existing brokerages. In addition, the challenge of effectively competing with multi-million-dollar companies in the fast-moving startup tech world never ends. Broker tech teams can fall into a trap of focusing on maintenance work versus innovation. Over time, code bases can erode, leaving brokers with tough decisions five years after launching a platform. Constant reinvention and reinvestment are a necessary, expensive requirement of a ground-up approach.

2. Acquire and Adapt

Instead of building from scratch, brokerage companies can purchase a tech company and adapt it to fit their business. Realogy did this with its $166 million 2014 purchase of ZipRealty and subsequent launch of ZapLabs (zaplabs.com). Re/Max followed this strategy with its 2018 acquisition of real estate brokerage marketing platform booj (booj.com), as did Howard Hanna in its 2014 acquisition of lead management firm One Cavo (onecavo.com). Highlighting how some companies adopt more than one strategy, Keller Williams Realty expanded its strategy to include this route when it acquired real estate mobile app developer Smarter Agent (smarteragent.com) in 2018.

- ▲ **Pros.** Purchasing a tech company to power brokerage growth has big competitive advantages. Brokers get a readymade tech platform and operational expertise that they can retool to their needs, which jumpstarts their tech efforts rather than starting from ground zero. This option, too, allows brokerages to control their own destiny.

- ▼ **Cons.** Adapting existing software to a brokerage is not easy. Brokerages must wrestle with transitioning current systems to a new one, which can be time-consuming and complicated. Rollout timelines are long and complicated, which can hamper innovation. Brokerages must find a way to both roll the tech out and continue to innovate — the fast-moving technology world does not stop. Firms employing this strategy must continually invest to keep up.

How to Optimize Tech Strategy in 7 Steps

Step 1 **Assess Current Technology and Set Goals**

First, brokerages need to take a hard look at their current technology. Take inventory of current systems, assess the effectiveness of each, and determine where the gaps and weaknesses are. The assessment should include how the tech package compares to market competitors and clear positioning. If brokerages with a strong technology offering are in the market or have plans to come, learn what they offer.

Step 2 **Clarify Tech Value Proposition**

Improving technology requires decisions, and most brokerages cannot implement technology everywhere in their business all at once. While brokerages should have a technology strategy that addresses all the brokerage technology landscape's seventy-eight categories presented in this chapter, they must prioritize some areas over others.

This involves getting clear on technology use, understanding company identity and competitive advantages, as well as agent audience and market positioning. These are critical to making effective technology decisions. When brokerages understand how they want to present themselves and where their competitive advantages lie, they can better determine which technology to focus on. Exercises in this step include:

- Conducting customer audience analysis to understand needs.
- Analyzing competition to clarify focus and strategy.
- Making a list of technology priorities.

This step also requires honest introspection. Brokerages should ask themselves if they have the resources, will, energy and money to make the necessary changes. If the answer is no, they should consider joining a firm that does.

Step 3 **Establish a Budget**

Brokerages confronting a modern technology strategy for the first time will have sticker shock as minimum annual spends go well into six figures. This high cost, which varies based on market and strategy, indicates the commitment technology requires.

Typical brokerage technology investments, for a fully integrated end-to-end technology platform that covers a significant portion of the consumer tech landscape, range from approximately $30 to $75 per agent per month. Brokerages who charge agents to recoup this investment typically have average agent tech fees of $75 per month. With a revenue-share agreement or negotiated discounts, brokerages can create a small surplus in some cases.

Step 4   Complete a Technology Landscape Exercise

After establishing goals, technology value proposition, and budget, brokers should review the brokerage tech landscape. Brokerages can use the technology landscape chart in this chapter to start devising strategies and technology options for each category. Remember that some options may span multiple categories in the chart. If possible, brokers should select technology that integrates or can work as an integrated system.

Step 5   Choose a Tech-Implementation Strategy

Only the biggest firms can consider a tech acquisition, equity investment or build in-house. Smaller brokerages must consider the other options. Brokerages should review all seven tech-implementation strategies in this chapter and determine which one, or combination, will provide them the quickest, most cost-effective and largest impact based on their budget and timeline. Multiple winning tech-implementation solutions exist but finding the right one requires good research and focused implementation.

Step 6   Vendor Exploration and Negotiation

This step involves researching and negotiating with tech vendor prospects. Brokerages will review proposals, negotiate deals and ultimately make your tech decisions in this step. Due diligence upfront will reduce headaches upon launch or implementation.

Step 7   Implementation, Testing and Rollout

Technology only performs well when companies implement it deeply into their operations and align it with a smart, overarching strategy. This stage involves implementing the technology, testing it to make sure it works and integrates where it needs to and a sustained, significant rollout to staff and agents supported by training, coaching and measurement.

3. Make an Equity Investment

Brokerage companies can also choose to make an equity investment in a tech platform. In addition to getting technology they want to tie into their businesses, they see their stake value increase as the tech company grows. Their interests are aligned.

Examples of firms employing this strategy include Howard Hanna and Long & Foster Real Estate's investment in Moxi Works (moxiworks.com), Realogy's investment in OJO Labs (ojo.me) and Notarize (notarize.com) and @properties' investment in Konverse (formerly Yapmo, konverse.com).

▲ **Pros.** Taking an equity investment is almost like buying a tech company without taking on all the financial and operational risk. Having influential and preferential treatment as a shareholder gives brokerages the luxury to suggest and strategically guide development. The investment also provides a public relations bump that can spur agent recruiting and retention. Companies investing in a technology firm can likely also negotiate lower prices.

▼ **Cons.** On the flip side, brokerages who make equity investments in a tech firm are not the sole decision-maker and cannot dictate every conversation or update. Tech companies still must innovate and allocate resources outside the investing firm's needs or wants. Also, in some cases, competitors invest in the same firm, mitigating any competitive advantage the tech could bring.

4. White-Label Tech

White-labeling technology, in which brokerages pay for a third-party platform but put their brand on it, can be a good solution. Brokerages get good out-of-the-box technology, their brand gets the credit with agents and consumers, and they have the flexibility to move on if things do not work out.

Examples include Daniel Gale Sotheby's International Realty's use of Real Estate Webmasters (realestatewebmasters.com) as its central hub under the name Dashboard. Another example is Weichert Realtors' white-label of Quantum Digital (quantumdigital.com) under the brand LeadLink.

▲ **Pros.** This strategy offers a plug-and-play solution that gives brokerages options and speed, allowing them to quickly adapt to a rapidly changing real estate technology landscape. White-labeling allows a firm to build a central hub; in some cases, this can be a single-sign-on environment, creating a simple, efficient workflow for agents and staff. When used in this way, this strategy gives brokerages the flexibility to swap out individual tech components, but keep the main tech hub intact.

▼ **Cons.** Not all systems play friendly with each other, and if brokerages are committed to white-labeling technology, they likely must commit to extra integration or customization work. The often relatively high costs per agent for these systems makes it a significant financial commitment – some tech firms charge a premium for white-labeling. In addition, brokerages are usually tied to the white-labeling company's product roadmap; in some cases, if they made extensive customizations, their version may need regular updates.

5. License Platform Software

Some firms find it best to go with real estate technology market leaders who offer a broad technology platform or that fully covers one or more technology categories. These platforms have strong, proven technologies, are fully focused on innovating in their category and the best of them focus on delivering top-notch customer service.

Examples of companies offering these types of platforms include Boston Logic (bostonlogic.com), BoomTown (boomtownroi.com), IDC Global (idcglobal.com), Inside Real Estate (insiderealestate.com) MoxiWorks, Real Estate Webmasters, SkySlope, dotloop and DocuSign.

Re/Max of Reading (Pennsylvania) leverages Boston Logic for its 225-agent base; The Keyes Company uses Inside Real Estate to power its firm; and Berkshire Hathaway HomeServices Drysdale uses IDC Global for its brokerage operating platform.

▲ **Pros.** Market-leading tech platform providers check many boxes and narrow down many tech decisions a brokerage needs to make. Each has its unique competitive advantages, and brokerages can consolidate a bulk of the brokerage tech landscape's seventy-eight categories into a few components with one of these systems. Many of these platforms constantly innovate to remain competitive, and if they do not, brokerages have the power (barring contract) to change. Licensing tech gives brokerages the luxury to focus on their core service of supporting agents and consumers. In addition, a few platforms offer some level of customization, which help brokers make the system a better fit.

Real Estate Companies Going Big on Tech

Keller Williams and Kelle

In 2017, Keller Williams Realty announced it was setting aside $1 billion to invest in building its own real estate technology and called itself a technology firm. Its tech hub, KW Labs, unveiled artificial intelligence-powered virtual assistant app Kelle to its agents in 2018. The technology uses big data from its agents, automates tasks for them and provides voice-activated support. In 2018, the company announced the acquisition of real estate mobile app developer Smarter Agent and a deal with artificial intelligence company KUNGFU.AI (kungfu.ai).

Windemere with Moxi Works

Seattle-based brokerage Windermere Real Estate built its technology solutions in-house and spun it off as a separate company in 2010 and rebranded it Moxi Works in 2014. Since then, it has picked up equity investments from other large regional brokerages including Long and Foster and Howard Hanna. These brokerages help guide product development, strategy and rollout of the platform, which includes a full brokerage and agent marketing stack, integrations with other popular technology and more.

▼ **Cons.** Agent adoption is always a concern. Fortunately, many of these firms have experience with this big pain point, so they may offer help. But adoption remains a challenge. In addition, brokerages are at the mercy of their vendor's feature roadmap. Tool training and support can be thin, as these firms often rely on a train-the-trainer support model.

Licensing costs can be difficult for a brokerage to absorb and they may need to offset them with agent technology fees. Longer-term contracts are common, so brokerages also take on some risk. If brokerages do not establish a deep partnership — where the vendor regularly updates technology, responds to their needs and requests and works in lockstep with them to innovate — the platform can become outdated, leaving brokerages with little recourse.

6. Integrate Best-of-Breed Vendors

Integrating multiple vendors into one platform can be challenging, but it allows brokerage to find what they like and reduces dependency on a single vendor. APIs have come a long way and cooperation is increasing across the industry among tech vendors. While smaller vendors may not check as many tech landscape category boxes as others, brokerages know the ones they do check perform well.

William Pitt-Julia B. Fee Sotheby's International Realty's new back-end platform provides an example. It integrates CRM Contactually (contactually.com), automated marketing tool Adwerx (adwerx.com), digital open house app Spacio (spac.io) and reputation management tool Lumentus (lumentus.com).

▲ **Pros.** Many of these solutions can wow agents, thanks to focusing on, and excelling in, a specific niche. Brokerages gain some agility with this strategy; for example, they can choose their preferred website vendor and also choose their favored CRM. They do not have to compromise, but can choose best-of-breed tools in the tech categories they care most about. This prevents brokerages from locking their tech fate with a larger technology company that has more features but may not innovate or update fast enough in specific categories.

▼ **Cons.** First of all, remaining current on the latest and greatest real estate tech is no small feat. It is difficult to determine what will actually work and is worth a bet and what would be a waste of time and money. Stability is also a risk in this strategy as brokerages can add too many distinct tools and lack a single core. Cost can be an issue for brokerages as they must maintain separate subscriptions with multiple firms. This also requires more management, as the brokerage has multiple relationships to maintain and lots of tools to monitor.

7. Implement General Technology

Non-industry-specific technology solutions are also an option. They generally lack real estate-specific capabilities, such as MLS integration, data types specific to real estate (properties, listings, showings, etc.) and connectivity to other rea-estate-specific applications. Fewer brokerages excel with this strategy as applying non-industry solutions to real estate requires technology skill.

Examples of these tools include Salesforce (salesforce.com), MailChimp (mailchimp.com), HubSpot (hubspot.com), Marketo (market.com), Microsoft Dynamics (dynamics.microsoft.com), Infusionsoft (infusionsoft.com) and WordPress (wordpress.com). Brokerages using this strategy include Realty Austin with its use of Saleforce and Hawaii Life with its use of Salesforce-based real estate CRM PropertyBase (now owned by Boston Logic, propertybase.com). These brokerages have multiple plugins and applications running in conjunction with their core technology.

- ▲ **Pros.** Brokerages using this strategy leverage massive technology investments and networks on a scale often not accessible in industry-specific tech. They usually include plug-and-play features, making integrations relatively straightforward. In some cases, non-industry-specific technology may be less expensive given the firms' great scale.

- ▼ **Cons.** These vendors do not have a real estate-specific focus or expertise, which can hamper the efficiency of some workflows. These companies often offer little to no support; for example, many resort to knowledgebases or networks of experts at high prices. In some cases, costs can be significantly higher than real estate-specific solutions. Agent adoption can also suffer as solutions not tailored to real estate can require more upfront learning, and many agents will not invest that time. Often, these tools require custom setup or adaptation for real estate, which takes financial resources, expertise and patience.

Takeaway

The time is now for brokerages to develop and implement a smart, holistic technology strategy (if they do not already have one). This will not be easy, cheap or immediate. It takes companywide effort. Firms that decide not to jump in will become increasingly obsolete. With technology becoming a core real estate component, brokerages now have primarily three options:

- Proactively reorient their firms around technology.
- Continue with a technology commitment.
- Sell.

> "Brokerages who invest in smart technology strategies will benefit from the streams of innovation flooding the industry."

The diversity of consumer needs and the array of different ways brokerages address them requires a technology solution that integrates many different types of technology products and services together, and also fits brokers' specific business models and brand.

Strategies will differ from brokerage to brokerage. Smaller firms do not have the funds to acquire or make huge equity investments in technology companies, but they can remain nimble and pick best-of-breed technology and outcompete larger firms in specific areas. Larger firms will enjoy scale and the benefits that come with it. Both can be successful.

Brokerages who invest in smart technology strategies will benefit from the streams of innovation flooding the industry. But it is neither cheap nor easy. They must invest capital, personnel, leadership, focus, training and support and accountability to successfully implement them.

Bold and clear action will allow brokerages to sustain, grow and evolve and remain significant players in real estate brokerage's next era.

Lead Contributors:

Travis Saxton
Travis has over ten years of experience in the residential real estate brokerage industry and serves as Senior Vice President of Technology for T3 Sixty. He previously worked at BombBomb as Vice President of Content Development and at REAL Trends as an author and Senior Technology Consultant. Travis can be reached at travis@t360.com.

Jack Miller
Jack has two decades of experience in the real estate industry and today serves as the President and CTO of T3 Sixty, where he heads up their consulting team. He previously worked as CTO of the Austin, Texas-based boutique brokerage The GoodLife Team, and prior to that he led a technology team with Keller Williams Realty. Jack can be reached at jack@t360.com.

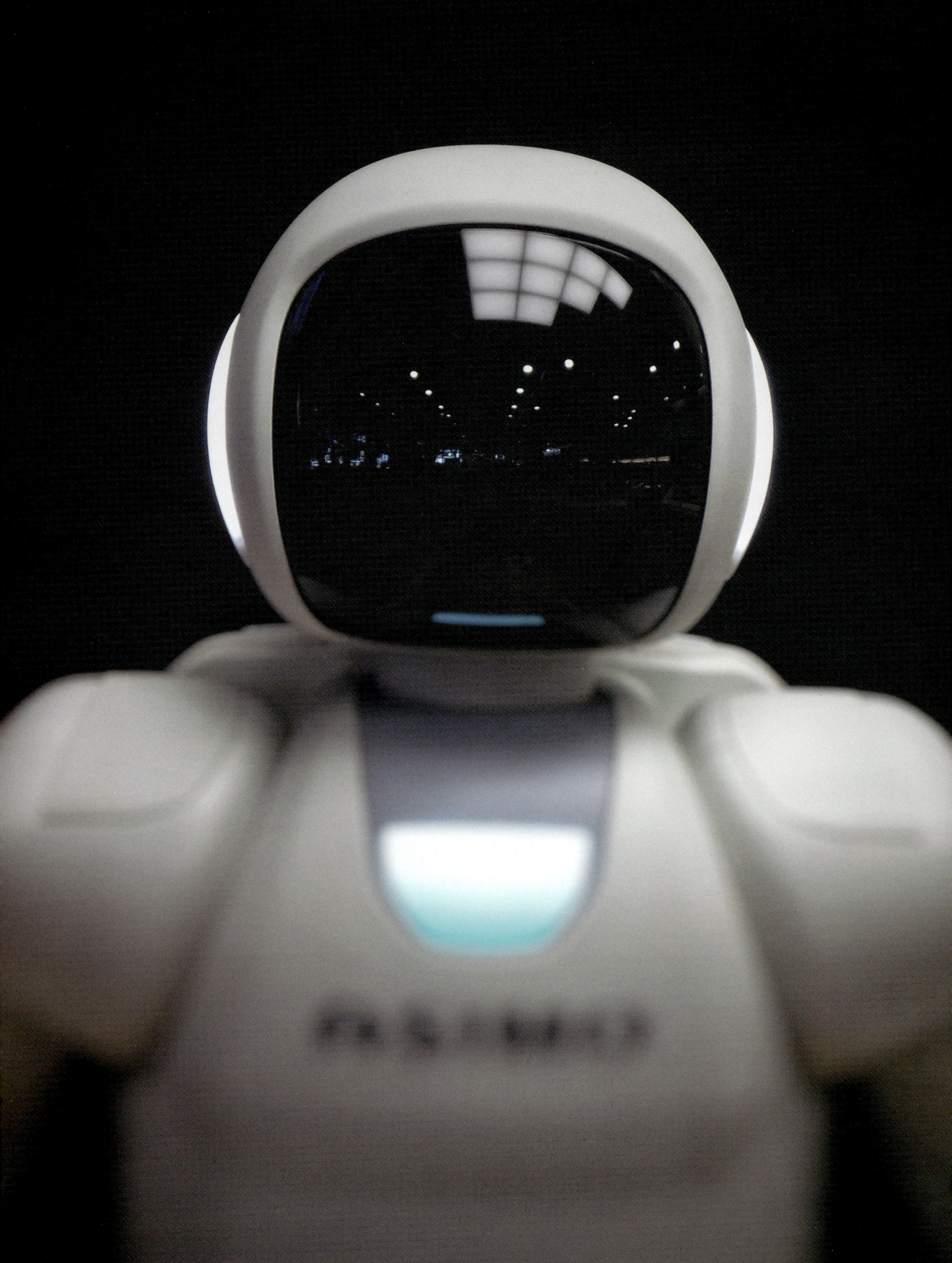

02 The Future of Real Estate Artificial Intelligence

Voice-Activated Search, Virtual Assistants, and Optimized Lead Conversion

Artificial intelligence (AI) has enormous potential to accelerate residential real estate brokerage technology and impact the way real estate professionals sell homes. Although already used in some real estate applications, the technology is still very young. Its great promise and novelty contributes to marketing hype, which makes understanding its full real estate industry potential difficult to determine.

The T3 Sixty team decided to help brokerage leaders more clearly understand what AI is, how existing industry tools currently leverage it and how it may evolve in the future.

> "I love the power and value technology offers but cringe every time an AI algorithm mismanages one of my tasks. AI is going to be a cursed blessing."
>
> Stefan Swanepoel

Defining AI

Some definitions restrict AI to a computer that can perfectly apply the nimble intelligence of a human (see insert "The Turing Test"). Many, including the T3 Sixty team, consider the machine-led optimization programs already present in many broker and agent tools full-fledged AI. AI not only makes many industry participants more efficient, it plays important roles in new brokerage business models.

Many AI elements described in this chapter already, or likely will soon, have a significant impact on homebuying and selling. They give real estate leaders another powerful tool to make operations more efficient, uncover new insights and improve service to both agents and consumers. AI will only become more useful as it evolves. Simply put, AI describes software that can mimic the human mind's problem-solving ability. A vast field with many applications and specialties, its applications give tools a variety of novel functionalities, including the ability to:

- Interpret visual and audio inputs.
- Communicate using natural language.
- Learn from experience.
- Develop optimization strategies.
- Make inferences and conclusions from data.
- Generalize and apply learning to new situations.

What AI is Not

Just because software appears smart does not mean it uses AI. For example, a real estate software might use a preprogrammed scoring algorithm to predict how likely a lead will become a client.

In this case, the tool might score leads based on whether they meet predefined criteria such as information completeness, specific inquiry keywords, the number of listings reviewed prior to inquiry, or other similar website- or app-usage information. The product might add up points it allocates to each action; leads with higher scores might be presented as better or hotter leads.

This is useful and powerful technology. However, the ability to perform additional and other preprogrammed routines does not constitute AI. AI can supplement these tools by using machine learning to determine the likelihood that leads will become clients, but the actions above do not fall within the definition of AI — it involves no software-led learning or problem-solving.

The Turing Test

Developed by computer scientist Alan Turing in the 1950s, the Turing Test is a test designed to determine a machine's ability to exhibit behavior that passes as human to human testers.

In the test, a human evaluator interacts with both a computer and another person and receives a response from each, but does not know which comes from which.

If the human judge cannot distinguish between the computer and the other human's responses, the computer system passes the Turing Test and, according to the test, demonstrates true artificial intelligence. Researchers debate whether AI systems have indeed passed the Turing Test or not.

1. Question asked of both participants.
2. Responses received from both.
3. Can the evaluator distinguish between the two?

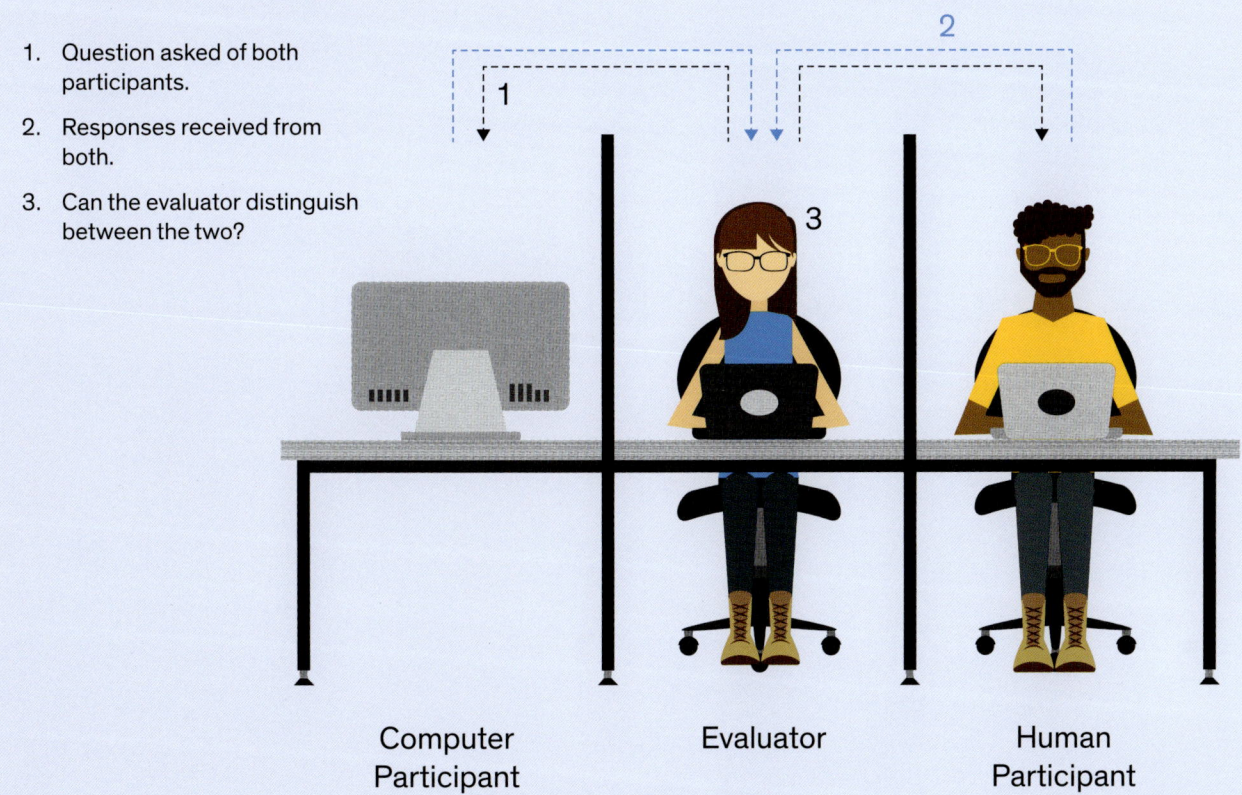

Computer Participant · Evaluator · Human Participant

Evaluate Real Estate Tech Providers Using AI

It is not easy to determine which platforms include true artificial intelligence. It can be difficult to tell AI programming apart from non-AI programming. To determine which systems have true AI, real estate pros should ask tech providers exactly how they use AI in their products and listen carefully to the answers. Here are a few questions to ask tech providers to help determine if their tool incorporates AI or not:

- Does your software interpret visual and audio inputs?
- If yes, is it communicating in natural language?
- Is it making conclusions from evidence it gathers?
- What kind of decisions is it making?
- Can it apply the lessons learned to new situations?

Next, brokerages and agents should ask to test the product with their own data in real time. When they load their own data into a system and quickly see results that satisfies their intelligence and intuition – when the system can quickly draw conclusions I love the power and value technology offers but cringe every time an AI algorithm mismanages one of my tasks. AI is going to be a cursed blessing., but on a larger scale or more accurately – then they may be looking at a product that leverages AI.

As with any software purchase, talking with existing customers is a good practice. Brokers and agents should determine whether the company's existing customers are trying to solve the same problem they are, how quickly and well are new data sources integrated into the product, how the product is implemented and trained, its measurable results and how it has improved over time.

Machine Learning and Deep Learning

A subset of AI, *machine learning,* describes a computer's ability to improve at a task while not explicitly programmed on how to do so. An algorithm – a set of computer instructions – that features machine learning can make increasingly accurate determinations or predictions by refining how it processes data. It adapts how it handles the data with no explicit human programming – instead, it *learns* by itself.

For example, a ridesharing company can use a machine learning algorithm to improve estimates of when and where rider demand will sharply increase based upon past trends and other data. In the real estate industry, AI systems can use machine learning to identify what room a listing photo represents, and even identify specific appliances and features. This automated data layer creates a richer search experience for real estate consumers.

A type of machine learning, *deep learning*, takes AI a step further. These systems stack AI algorithms on top of each other, creating an *artificial neural network* that gives an AI system more subtle, powerful self-learning capabilities. This multilayered system, with multiple connections and feedback loops, approximates the way a human brain works. An AI system uses deep learning to decipher specific features in an image, for example.

> " ... creating an artificial neural network that gives an AI system more subtle, powerful self-learning capabilities ... "

Knowing When Products Use AI

If a chatbot provider claims that its tool uses AI, ask how it improves itself with data. If the company notes that its programmers constantly improve the tool's ruleset rather than describing how the software self-adjusts, a robust AI system is most likely not in use.

If a technology provider claims to use machine learning, ask how it trains the software to make decisions, assessments or take actions. In an image-recognition tool, for example, ask the provider how it trains the algorithm. If responses include mention of "training data" the system uses to optimize its conclusions – and they get more accurate over time – it likely uses AI (see insert for more).

Assessing AI Tools

An AI system is only as useful as the quality of data it runs on. Technology providers with AI platforms must intensely focus on their data quality, as AI only interprets the world through the data it receives.

Ask AI tool providers if the software will be trained with data from inside their business? If they answer yes, a quality tool may be far off – successful AI systems typically require millions of data sets from different sources to provide meaningful, useful results.

If early customers of a company developing an AI system, brokerage leaders should know the product will not likely be immediately useful – or it may not be useful at all. Users should ask if the system will use real estate industry feedback data from other brokerages and agents to train the system. A good real estate AI system will do this.

> " A good real estate AI system will do this."

If brokers ask software companies claiming to use AI about the data sources they use and they respond, "We have our own data we use to train our system," they know these systems use a limited subset of the information needed to train a top-notch AI tool, and might question how much AI they really use.

Brokers should also ask about which big data sources are integrated into the AI system. For example, an AI-infused lead scoring system would likely integrate with a broker's CRM, email and phones to incorporate lead-interaction data that influences conversion rates. Keep in mind: An effective AI system requires a ton of high-quality data.

Real Estate AI Applications

Real estate has an abundance of data, and, as should be clear from the previous section: good AI systems love data. Because large amounts of quality data are so critical to the quality of AI systems, the more they have, the more useful they are. AI applications continuously improve as they process new data and learn from each output.

A variety of AI applications already have a presence in the industry, including lead scoring and scrubbing, automated property valuations, personalized services, transaction management, virtual assistants and home search.

Lead Scoring and Scrubbing

Some existing AI-enabled real estate products help score and respond to leads. These systems compare the search behavior, contact response patterns, big data related to finances and life events and more of new leads with the same elements of leads who became clients. From that data-rich, nonlinear comparison, the software predicts which new leads are likely to convert or most ready to transact.

Because the data these systems use is so large and diverse, it is often impossible for humans to track or understand how the tools make predictions, but the outcomes should speak for themselves. A good system will beat most human analysis, and also continually improve over time.

An AI-infused lead system might handle additional tasks. For example, it might pass what it deems as the best leads directly to agents while putting leads who it thinks have longer transaction timelines or show less transaction promise on an automated followup campaign.

These systems may also determine the specific content and tone of messages that specific leads will respond to best based on their profiles.

These AI systems can surface leads who agents may otherwise have dismissed because they initially assessed them as low value based on the surface information they had. Additionally, an AI tool can effectively incubate longer-tail leads who may initially not be ready to talk to an agent; when their behavior or other big data signals indicate they are a hotter lead, the system can alert an agent. An AI tool's incubation actions can include leaving a voicemail or another message to maintain a connection or deliver requested information.

These systems can cultivate revenue-generating relationships, without a brokerage or agent lifting a finger until the end of the process to close the deal. Less leads fall through the cracks with these AI-infused tools.

Property Valuations and Data

Some tools that make automated property valuations use AI to refine the accuracy of their assessments. Some companies even use AI to interpret listing photos to create data beyond fields entered in the MLS—such as property condition—to develop automated property value estimates.

AI valuation tools often make valuations more accurate with additional data from existing sources and new data from other sources without a human programmer involved. AI can determine whether manually-entered property information is incorrect based on comparisons with other sources. An AI-powered valuation can include not just information about the property, but information around it including the neighborhood, points of interest, and demographic and environmental data. AI valuations can also assess the relative heat or chill of a market and incorporate a buyer's timing goals to develop an optimal valuation based on a buyer's specific needs. Existing AI valuation products have these

Data using existing technologies   *Data boost through use of artificial intelligence*

Illustrating AI's Power

To visualize the impact of AI on real estate, consider the amount data that can be extracted from a room photo. The above visual shows two different types of data collection. The first, yellow, showcases existing data collected on a room photo. For example, in a kitchen existing technology may have recorded that there is hardwood floors, or upgraded appliances. Overall, data is limited and remains surface-level, without too much specification (i.e. what type of hardwood floors are in place).

With artificial intelligence and machine learning comes in, output data includes visualization, internet search and data analysis. The output: walnut hardwood floors, Samsung refrigerator with freezer, etc. In some cases, it will identify additional data on existing items. In other cases, it will identify new data.

Existing Data
- Open Kitchen
- Upgraded Appliances
- Hardwood Floors

AI Enhanced Data
- Open Kitchen
- Upgraded Appliances (incl. Samsung Fridge)
- Walnut Hardwood Floors
- Tile Backsplash, Stone, Unique Pattern
- Standalone Stove/Oven, GE Brand
- White Cabinets, Recessed Handles
- Waterfall Island with White Marble Top

features. Data coverage and quality will continue to improve, which will increase these valuations' accuracy and the business models and actions they enable.

Direct Buyers rely on these AI-powered tools to make offers on homes in as soon as twenty-four hours of receiving a seller request. These firms, such as Opendoor and Offerpad, must quickly provide sellers offers that meet their business goals and do not grossly overprice or underprice a property. For more on the Direct Buyer model, see Trend No. 2 in the *2018 Swanepoel Trends Report*, "Enter the Direct Buyer."

In the future, AI tools will be able to include a property's condition and curb appeal into valuation estimates and listing recommendations from drone footage and other visual information. If a property or neighborhood appears run down and data indicates its trajectory is heading downward, AI systems can recognize that and incorporate it into estimates, often quicker and more accurately than humans can. Expect the gap between the sophistication and accuracy of human and AI software valuations to shrink.

> "AI tools will likely be able to assess the condition of a listing by analyzing photos, comparing the listing against current design trends, and creating personalized recommendations for repair and remodeling, including connections with service providers."

Personalized Products and Services

Financial services companies already use AI to tailor loan parameters and suggest additional products most appropriate to individual borrowers based on profiles the system creates from consumer financial data. These AI tools integrate credit data from multiple sources and analyze and act upon it while conforming to company policies. They can explain decisions and actions, explain exclusions and eligibility decisions, price products and underwrite deals subject to conditions, and provide a list of conditions applicants must meet to receive a loan.

These systems can also analyze consumer debt and suggest debt-consolidation strategies borrowers might employ to lower costs and improve their debt portfolio. AI tools can now handle complicated financial evaluation and decision-making, once the purview of top-notch, and expensive, call center staff.

"Real estate brokers and agents have many highly specialized virtual assistant programs to choose from today."

Smoother Transactions

Transaction management tools with AI already automatically identify missing documents at various points in the transaction and alert professionals of dangers to a smooth transaction. AI tools are also starting to uncover errors in completed documents and flag the parts of contracts that require broker review.

In the future, AI systems will access various data sources during the transaction process to quickly evaluate if other transaction impediments exist, such as property liens or credit changes, and calculate the amount of risk a deal carries. Eventually, AI tools will learn to assess many other factors to determine transaction risk. They will likely identify risk factors in transactions that brokers, agents and loan officers have not considered before.

These systems will also know what information and documents transaction participants need and send them for review or signature at the appropriate time. They will know when to prefill information in those documents and know to check with the broker or agent when uncertain about something, just the way a human assistant would.

A Real Virtual Assistant

Real estate brokers and agents have many highly specialized virtual assistant programs to choose from today. Some of those systems that include AI can monitor emails for appointment language (i.e. "Let's grab lunch next week") and then suggest meeting times with a client based on an agent's calendar availability. They can book and verify the meeting all without an agent involved. This removes the time-consuming hassle of setting appointments.

In addition, agents can invite an AI virtual assistant via email to their phone meetings. The AI system dials in and listens, taking notes and identifying important moments. It can also dial into meetings for which brokers or agents are double-booked and cannot attend. It can even listen to their in-person meetings via a mobile app, and take notes on those meetings.

Another AI virtual assistant — more limited but still useful — leverages a branch of AI called *natural language processing* that allows a computer to read, understand and interpret email content and update existing CRMs based on email signatures.

In the future, agents' AI virtual assistants will ensure that brokers and agents' online advertisements match current listing information and alert them to wrong or out-of-date information.

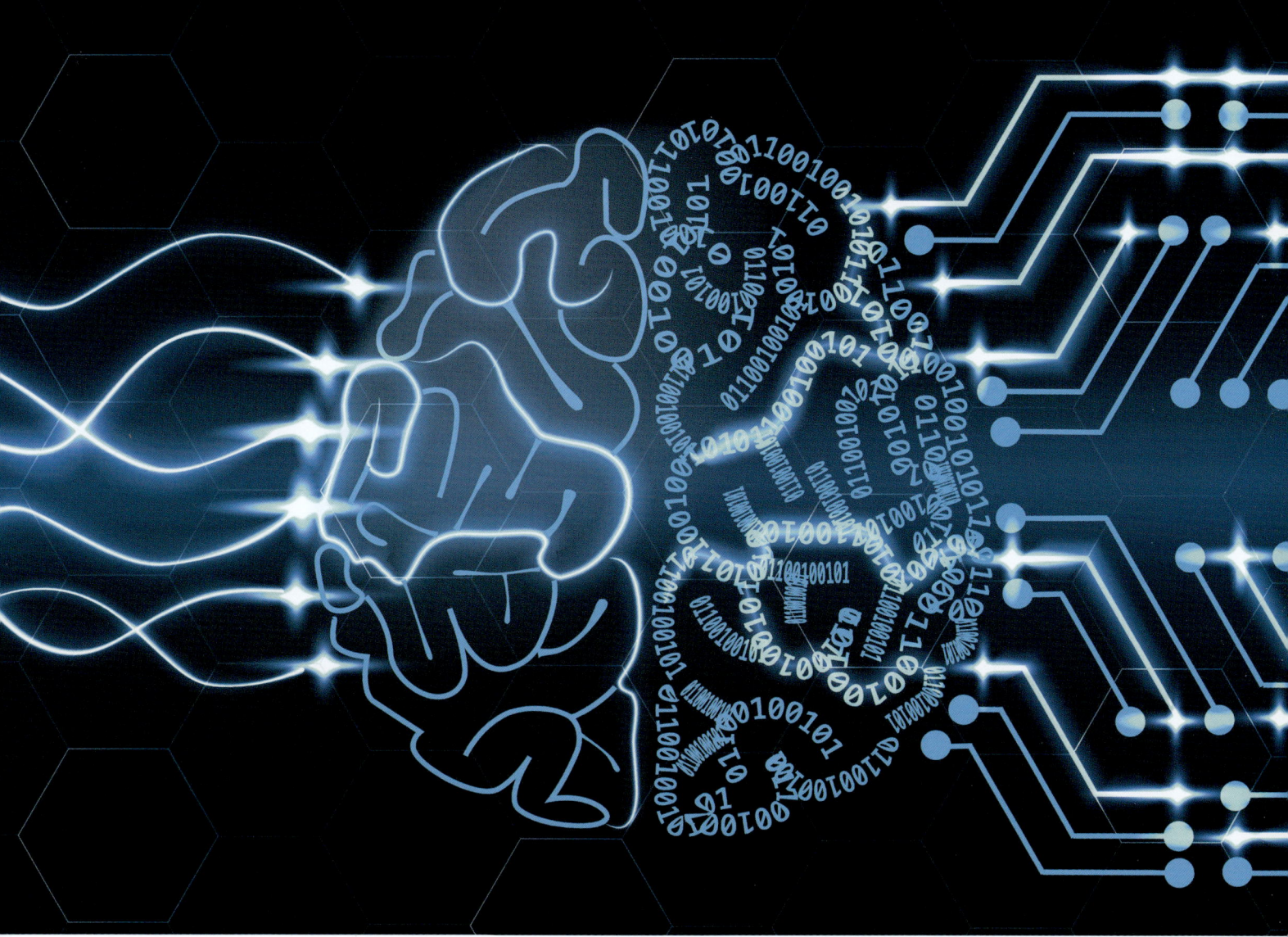

These tools will take many of the simple, repetitive tasks brokers and agents must complete off their plates. For example, an AI virtual assistant could place paid listing advertisements on brokers and agents' behalf, on sites where they typically place ads for certain listing types. These tools can incorporate what brokers and agents have done in the past — or what the AI predicts may be more successful in the future.

AI virtual assistants will no doubt perform many of the time-consuming and repetitive tasks brokers and agents do today. The above are just a few examples.

Better Home Search

Brokers, agents and consumers have an increasing number of voice-based AI applications that promise to help them with real estate tasks, but those currently available certainly would not pass the Turing Test. However, conversations with future versions will feel more human than computer-like, which, in addition to improving functionality for brokers and agents, will greatly improve the automated, voice-activated home search experience for consumers.

For example, buyers could ask an AI virtual assistant to "Search for two-bedroom homes I can afford," and the system would know to reference or query their financial information to assess their budget for a home. The virtual assistant might search areas previously searched rather than listings near the consumer's current location.

Search results would account for users' specific circumstances — the people they live with, their current lifestyle choices and needs, their favorite places or similar places they like elsewhere, proximity to friends and family, listings they liked or lingered on in previous searches, and much more. Unlike agents, an AI virtual assistant will not have to ask for information for buyer context — users could allow the app to access social media information, location history and other online information, and the system would understand how to interpret it in a home search.

AI will curate information so buyers do not get overwhelmed. Buyers will ask a virtual assistant for additional information about a property and, if the information is included in the listing description, photos or other integrated data sources, the AI assistant could answer questions and automate parts of the search experience for both buyers and agents.

Direct Buyer Model

Firms using the Direct Buyer business model (also known as iBuyers) already use AI tools to generate short-notice offers on homes; site unseen. These companies will increasingly use AI to assess property condition, validate valuations, manage the logistics and scheduling for home repair and maintenance, manage transaction risk and determine the optimum time to sell. For more information on the Direct Buyer model, see Trend No. 2 in the *2018 Swanepoel Trends Report*, "Enter the Direct Buyer."

Future Applications

> "Providing information from databases and photos is just the tip of the AI-conversation iceberg."

Providing information from databases and photos is just the tip of the AI-conversation iceberg. In 2018, Google stunned the world with a demonstration of its Duplex chatbot that called businesses to ask questions and schedule appointments — responding and sounding human-like while doing so. See a demonstration of AI in the Google Assistant app at the search giant's 2018 Google I/O conference (bit.ly/IOkeynote).

In the future, a similar AI system could leave messages, take answers from callbacks and deliver those answers to buyers. It could coordinate with all parties to set showings and adapt appropriately when a human on the other end of the line answers in unexpected ways. It is possible that many information-based conversations brokerages and agents have with service providers, and in some cases, consumers, will be done through their AI virtual assistants who will not often need human assistance.

When applied to real estate, an AI tool with similar capabilities could make calls on behalf of an agent to set a photo shoot or schedule other service providers. The same is true, of course, for applications geared toward consumers – brokerages and agents may not know that the caller asking for information on a specific listing may be an AI virtual assistant.

In the real estate investment trust (REIT) and commercial sectors, AI tools will analyze new listings that come on the market for portfolio fit. One day, an AI system may buy and sell properties itself to rebalance a portfolio just as current stock broker investment systems rebalance stocks and other investment vehicles.

> "AI, of course, will continue to evolve."

AI, of course, will continue to evolve. AI systems will fit more situations and pull in more data; they will also become more accurate. In some cases, humans might not know they are interacting with an AI system.

AI's Biggest Challenges

AI is immensely powerful and works, in large part, without human oversight. This is its big appeal and strength, but also a liability. The lack of active human involvement in AI tasks and processes comes with significant challenges, as the relevancy, quality and accuracy of input data determines the quality of AI output. If the AI system receives poor data, it will deliver inaccurate conclusions. In some cases, it can be difficult for humans to realize the inaccuracy or recognize it only long after the fact.

Humans might not even know when a system goes off track because many AI tools operate without humans knowing exactly how they work. This requires users to continually measure the outcome AI tools deliver to ensure they remain useful, relevant and productive.

AI systems also bring up important questions around privacy and security. As current AI systems already use sensitive information and will increasingly do so in the future, ensuring personal data remains safe and private will be an ongoing challenge.

AIs Need High-Quality Data

When it comes to real estate, AI's tenuous connection to the real world is its biggest weakness. AI systems need high-quality information to

deliver accurate, useful conclusions. In some cases, this means that AI systems need more information; in all cases, useful AI systems require accurate data.

For example, rather than waiting for an individual brokerage or agent to order a drone flight for a listing, some companies are flying drones to cover entire neighborhoods. This provides more complete data for an AI system to analyze area coverage. As almost everyone knows, Google gathers street-view photos by periodically driving areas with its own vehicles. In the near future, delivery vehicles and taxis — and possibly even consumer vehicles — may gather this imagery in addition to noise, air quality and other data. Smart-home sensors will become part of this data network managed by AI systems.

At some point, data or information companies will likely subsidize advanced imagery and information-gathering in exchange for permission to use that content as part of their analysis and data products.

Important questions arise here. Who owns the data? Does it matter? Who monitors the systems for safe use? The real estate industry has taken some initial steps to address the issues surrounding AI, by creating or licensing the information and creating data standards. Still, a full-fledged AI regulatory system remains far off. The Wild West of AI will need laws and a sheriff to enforce them.

Privacy

Privacy legislation may be a much larger hurdle for AI, to cross if the European Union's General Data Protection Regulation (GDPR) is a sign of things to come. It is not clear yet whether privacy concerns will significantly hamper AI growth or if governments and industries will wait to develop rules and guidelines after the initial flurry of AI innovation. The big privacy questions related to AI currently include:

- Will consumers opt-out of sharing data that AI systems need to operate? Will they even have that ability?

- Will the burden of complying with new laws, including a required opt-in for new data uses, be too much for AI companies to overcome? Will a restriction of available data hamper AI tool functionality?

- Will GDPR-like data retention limitations limit AI applications that need historical data?

These important questions may not have answers for many years. AI innovators, and industry practitioners hoping to use their systems, must closely watch the evolution of privacy legislation.

Security

Ensuring that AI systems have sufficient security is another significant challenge for AI. When AI systems gather personal data — whether through voice, bank records or other sources — they have an incredible amount of personal information that is vulnerable to hacking.

Hackers could issue malicious voice commands to an AI assistant or computer. Or they could steal identities and use internet-of-things devices to order goods, unlock smart locks or steal an AI-enabled car. As AI connects to many big data sources, and users grant AI software access to personal information, users' security risks increase.

Steering Issues

If an AI system is used in the real estate search process, it could contribute to steering, influencing homebuyers in ways that discriminate on identity, race and other demographic factors. This could occur without brokers', agents' or consumers' knowledge, nevertheless could still violate the Fair Housing Act, which prohibits real estate brokerages and agents from steering buyers to specific areas based on their demographics.

Will brokers or agents be responsible if an AI system involved in the real estate search process unintentionally contributes to steering? How does the industry monitor and prevent this?

Just as many cities and states have banned employers from asking job candidates about their salary history to remedy gender pay gaps, if a real estate AI tool assesses historical data as a basis for future recommendations, it may play a part in contributing to housing inequality. Who bears responsibility in this scenario?

The industry will need to answer these important questions before AI real estate tools can really take off.

> "Will brokers or agents be responsible if an AI system involved in the real estate search process unintentionally contributes to steering?"

Takeaway

The potential for AI to make brokers, agents and consumers more efficient and uncover valuable insights that improve operations is great. Indeed, many AI systems already do this. And many more are in the works.

The application of AI in the residential real estate brokerage industry is still early. Many applications coming online are just ramping up – their power and utility will become clearer as they mature.

AI also cannot foster the relationships and trust buyers and sellers need as a part of the real estate process. It cannot provide comfort and confidence to the buyer, it cannot appeal to the emotions of the seller on behalf of a buyer and it cannot judge people and situations as needed to negotiate.

> "With AI's great promise, some wonder whether it will replace real estate agents. The short answer is no. AI cannot yet fully interact with the physical world – it will not get homes ready for showings any time soon."

Time will tell if it will take over more nuanced human tasks, but, for now and the near future, AI will supplement residential real estate professionals, giving them powerful tools that improve efficiency and uncover valuable business insights.

One day in the future AI may power a robot that takes a final look around a house before a showing, wipe the cat hair off the couch and prepare fresh-baked cookies. Until then, brokerages and the real estate agents that serve homebuyers and sellers will remain overwhelmingly human.

Lead Contributor:

Matt Cohen

Matt has been a real estate industry technologist for twenty-three years. He specializes in strategic planning, MLS consolidation and security audits. He served as Chief Technologist at Clareity Consulting before CoreLogic (NYSE: CLGX) acquired the company. He is now a Principal, Product Manager at CoreLogic Real Estate Solutions. The views expressed in this article are those of Matt and T3 Sixty and do not necessarily reflect the views of Matt's employer, CoreLogic. Matt can be reached at macohen@corelogic.com.

Bonus Supplement
Examples of Real Estate AI Tools

ojōlabs
(Ojo Labs)

Launched in 2015, Austin, Texas-based Ojo Labs offers real estate brokers and agents an AI-based digital assistant that responds to leads using natural language via text message. It connects with consumers on behalf of a brokerage or agent who discover Ojo through advertising, or from a broker or agent directly.

Ojo is designed to provide consumers real estate data and insights before they are ready to talk with an agent. To minimize confusion, the system notifies consumers that it is not an actual person. "The tool fills the void for consumers searching for a home online who are ready for more information, but not ready to engage with an agent," says Ojo Labs co-founder and CEO, John Berkowitz.

Ojo Labs built the tool with AI so that it constantly evolves and learns through human interactions. The startup first seeded the algorithm with 14 million real estate conversations. It has since run hundreds of thousands of conversations, learning from each one.

When it receives a message, the tool breaks it down into tiny components, determining whether the text is part of an existing conversation or a new one entirely. If the inquiry is part of an existing thread, the tool knows to search for contextual information to pull into the chat. Because it plugs into an MLS database, it also has access to inventory information, in which it derives additional information from relevant listings and photos.

Ojo slowly builds a profile for each consumer, while developing a specific conversation style, and aims to tailor its responses to each user's unique needs and desires. When consumers' behavior indicates they may need an agent's assistance, or they request to speak with an agent, the tool connects them to an agent and, if consumers agree, shares their profile.

While powered by AI, the tool does not fly without a net. Ojo Labs has a team of over 180 full-time employees in the US and St. Lucia who provide 24/7 human backup when the machine gets stuck in a conversation. Each time the human team steps in, the tool catalogues how the conversation progresses and learns for future applications.

In late 2017, Ojo Labs signed an enterprise deal with Realogy. It is currently working on rolling out the tool to Realogy agents across multiple markets.

(First.io)

Founded in 2016, First.io (first.io) builds products powered by AI machine learning algorithms that help real estate agents prioritize conversations with people who are likely to lead to business. It uses data from 214 million U.S. individuals and 145 million US households to help rank which agents' contacts will sell sooner than others.

Agents dump all their contacts into the startup's tool – phone and email contacts, LinkedIn, CRM – and then it goes to work. It matches contacts to property addresses and gives contacts a Seller Score.

Higher Seller Scores mean the contacts have a higher propensity to sell in the next twelve months. A quarter of the homeowners that score in the top 5 percent of First.io's model sell within the next 12 months, according to First.io.

The tool also assesses the strength of relationships agents have with their specific contacts based on their type and frequency of interactions. The firm combines this assessment with the Seller Score to prioritize which agents should reach out to next. When it determines that a contact may be ready for a conversation, it pings agents with targeted recommendations.

The firm's AI continues to learn and improves its predictions every month, says First co-founder and CEO Mike Schneider. The firm sells its tool to brokerages, agents and teams.

SKYSLOPE (SkySlope)

Digital transaction management platform SkySlope uses an AI machine learning algorithm to automate tasks brokers and agents have to complete in a transaction such as assessing the forms and items needed for specific transactions, filling out information the system reads from uploaded documents, adding people to the transaction based on uploaded documents.

The firm's transaction assistant, Skye, learns what disclosures and document types go with specific properties. For example, some counties require asbestos disclosures. If Skye detects the word asbestos in an uploaded document and the listing falls within one of the counties that requires the disclosure, it automatically appends the disclosure to the transaction.

SkySlope also uses the AI in its enterprise broker and agent transaction coordination service, SkyTC. The AI system analyzes and organizes the emails of SkySlope's transaction coordinators to streamline workflows and establish efficient priorities.

By reading the email, the system predicts what SkyTC coordinators should do with the email and suggests an action. They can accept the suggestion or modify it. In both cases, the AI algorithm learns so the accuracy of its suggestions increase over time.

FOLLOW THE MONEY

An update on the number 1 trend of the *2018 Swanepoel Trends Report*

Researched and compiled by
Michele Conn, SVP M&A, T3 Sixty

Real Estate Tech Funding in 2018

With a total of $2.2 billion in funding, investment in real estate technology hit an all-time high in 2017, nearly double 2016's total. This made it the top trend in the *2018 Swanepoel Trends Report.*

Real estate tech investment is still a huge trend. 2018 funding through the third quarter is already 86 percent of the full-year 2017 amount. If the pace continues, 2018 funding will end 14 percent over 2017's total.

2018 funding through the third quarter stands at over $1.9 billion. If the fourth quarter continues along the same trajectory, full-year 2018 funding will reach $2.5 billion, setting another industry funding record.

Total Residential Real Estate Tech Funding

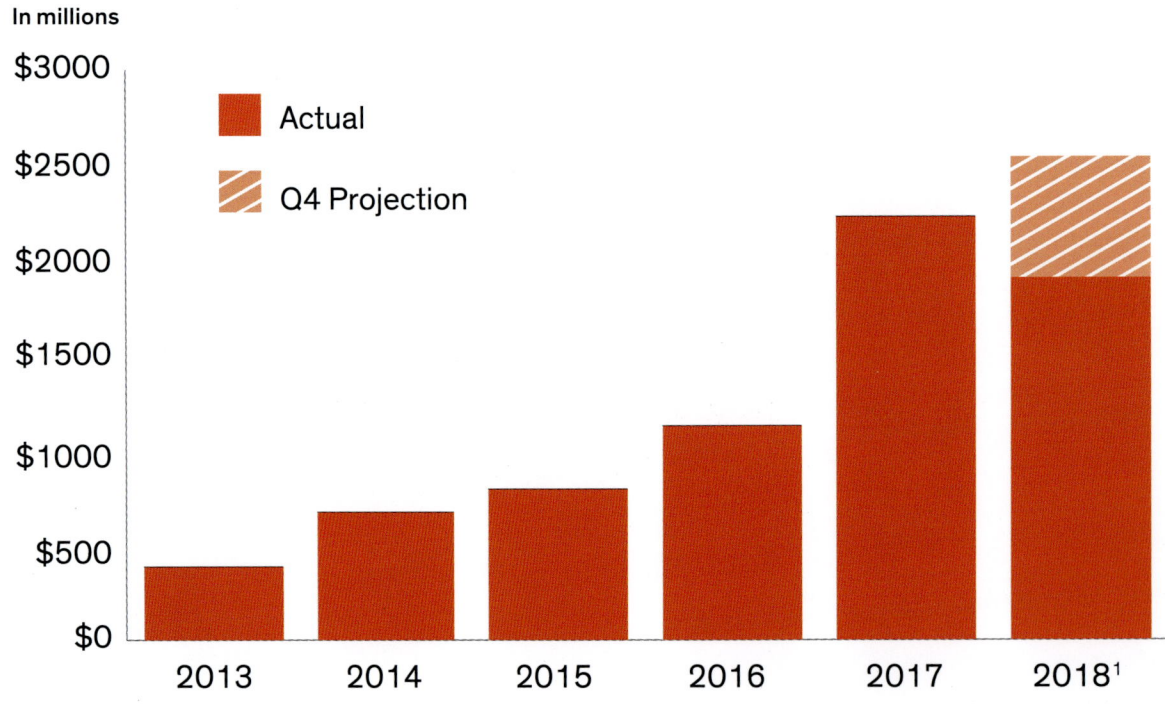

Source: T3 Sixty with Crunchbase data
[1] Through November 5.

Funding Dollars (Left) and Number of Companies Funded by Stage (Right)

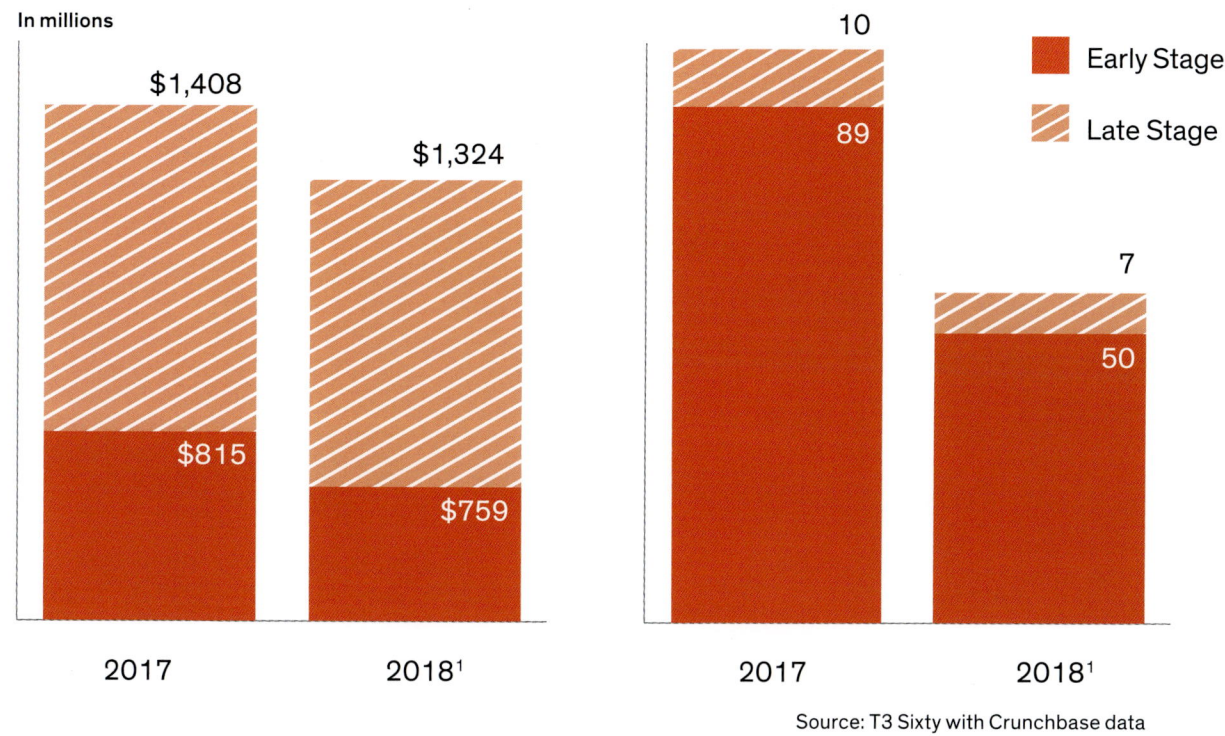

Source: T3 Sixty with Crunchbase data
[1] Through November 5.

Investments By Stage

Through the third quarter 2018 real estate technology funding has followed the 2017 trends in terms of funding by stage of companies. In both 2017 and 2018, 60 to 70 percent of funding dollars were directed to companies raising Series C or later funding rounds. Late-stage funding is often associated with companies focused on scaling and maturing their businesses. In 2018 through the third quarter, Opendoor and Compass alone represent 85 percent of the industry's late-stage funding.

Early-stage funding, marked by angel rounds through Series B rounds, is often used to help companies validate and establish their product and grow the initial business. Typically, early-stage funding rounds are smaller as these companies and their investors experiment with new products and business models. For example, the average funding by early-stage company was $11.6 million in the first three quarters of 2018 and $9.2 million in 2017.

The ratio of companies funded in late stages versus those funded in early stages held steady from 2017 to the first three quarters of 2018 with approximately 90 percent of companies funded classified as early stage. However, the number of early-stage companies funded in 2018 dropped notably from 2017. However, that difference may become less stark with funding events in fourth quarter 2018.

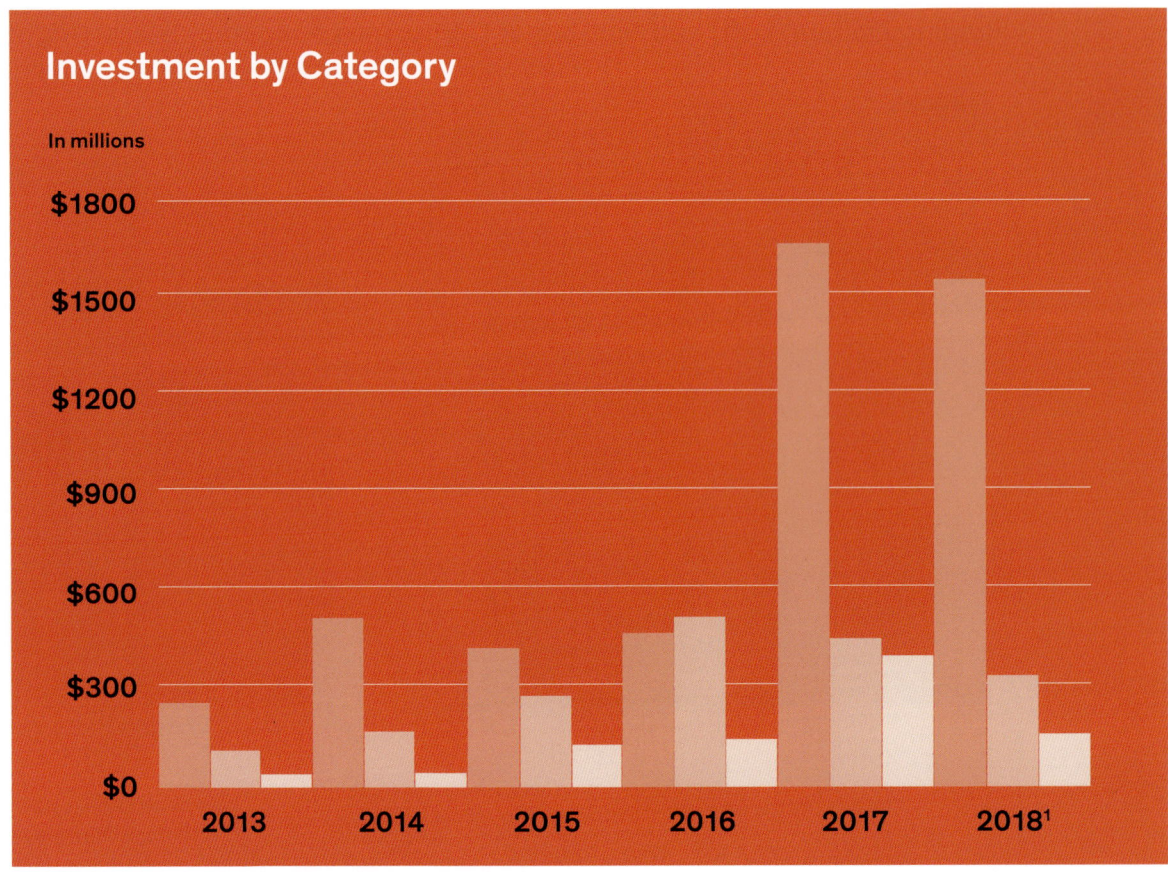

Source: T3 Sixty with Crunchbase data]
[1] Through Nov. 5.

Investments By Category

Residential technology continued to lead funding in the real estate sector in the first three quarters of 2018.

Investment has heavily focused on tech-centric brokerage models, even exceeding the high level reached in 2017. Investors poured in nearly $1.3 billion in just three companies in this category: Opendoor raised a huge $725 million in two late-stage funding rounds, the latter led substantially by SoftBank Vision Fund (softbank-ia.com/vision-fund). Compass also continued to raise funds in 2018 with a $400 million Series F raise from Qatar Investment Authority (qia.qa) and SoftBank Vision Fund. LL Funds invested $150 million of debt and equity in Direct Buyer Offerpad (offerpad.com).

Although on a smaller scale than tech-centric brokerage models, rental technology companies in the residential category have raised substantial amounts of money in 2018 through the third quarter. Bungalow (bungalow.com) leapt into the co-living space with a $64 million Series A and debt raise, led by Khosla Ventures (kholslaventures.com). ApartmentList (apartmentlist.com) and Zumper (zumper.com) raised $50 million and

$46 million Series C rounds, respectively, to compete in the crowded rental category.

Investment in the commercial space is on track to be slightly lower in 2018 than 2017, primarily due to a decrease in investor crowdfunding platforms. Investor crowdfunding platforms have garnered $75.8 million in 2018 through the third quarter after accounting for more than $100 million every year since 2015. Among investor crowdfunding investment, PeerStreet (peerstreet.com) raised a $29.5 million Series B and newcomer Skyline AI (skyline.ai) raised a $21M Series A. Commercial data, search and analytics provider Reonomy (reonomy.com) led the commercial company funding with a $46 million Series C, led by SAP-affiliated Sapphire Ventures.

After a high point in 2017 driven by a handful of large, late-stage investments, mortgage technology funding is tracking much lower in 2018. Despite that trend, Cloudvirga (cloudvirga.com), provider of mortgage processing and workflow technology, raised a $50 million in Series C funding.

The Shift

T3 Sixty's research indicates that the real estate tech funding trend has reached, or is near, its peak. The amount of annual real estate tech funding is expected to decrease in 2019 and 2020.

A massive amount in the 2018 funding cycle came from the Softbank Vision Fund. The SoftBank Vision Fund is different from SoftBank's corporate investing arm, SoftBank Capital. The SoftBank Vision Fund combines SoftBank's own funding with money raised from outside investors, including Saudi Arabia's Public Investment Fund, Abu Dhabi's Mubadala Investment Company, Apple, Sharp, Qualcomm, Foxconn and others.

The SoftBank Vision Fund, alone, provided $800 million, or 42 percent, of the real estate tech funding through the first three quarters of 2018. This went to just two companies: Compass and Opendoor. The SoftBank Vision Fund also invested $450 million in Compass in 2017, in its debut investment.

Both Compass and Opendoor are current industry high flyers but their valuations have risen so sharply that higher-valuation exits is becoming increasingly unlikely. Expect these companies to continue to make bold moves in 2019 and 2020 as they spend their vast war chests.

"Expect these companies to continue to make bold moves in 2019 and 2020."

01 Mapping the Real Estate Brokerage Landscape

A Comparison of the Industry's Predominant Business Models

As technology matures and venture capital flows in the residential real estate brokerage industry, new business models are emerging and growing at unprecedented rates. This leaves established real estate brokers perplexed and unsure how to respond. Newer models, flush with venture capital funds, are pushing full throttle forward, making it tough to keep track of who is playing what hand and how. There is no easy way to organize the industry's many brokerage business models into a clear structure, but that is what T3 Sixty has done.

This chapter presents the first comprehensible comparison and analysis of the residential real estate brokerage industry's predominant business models.

Brokerage Business Model Landscape

After researching and dissecting the industry's predominant brokerage companies in many different ways, it became evident that a complete comparison would not fit cleanly into a single box or grid. After many hours of thought and debate, the T3 Sixty team developed a comparison framework that it feels effectively compares the industry's the many different brokerage models. Before diving in, it will help to understand the thought process behind it and its structure.

First, T3 Sixty distilled five core brokerage business model elements and then identified the two opposing aspects of each element. The five brokerage elements (with their two opposing aspects in parentheses) are:

- **Agent Compensation** (Employee Agents—Independent Agents)

- **Technology** (Insourced—Outsourced)

- **Brokerage Operating Capital** (Bigger—Smaller)

- **Fee Structure** (Low Fee, Flat Fee—Commission, Sliding Scale)

- **Consumer Relationship** (Average—High)

> "As the ground shifts from under it, new business models are jockeying with legacy companies for leadership in real estate's next era."

The T3 Sixty team then identified twelve well-known brokerage companies that represent the industry's predominant business models. Obviously, there are many more companies, some whose business models vary in different ways. Many are, however, fundamentally the same (from a business model point of view). To make the comparison easier to digest, we used representatives for the industry's primary different types of business models. The brokerage companies used to illustrate the different brokerage business models are:

- Compass
- eXp Realty (NASDAQ: EXPI)
- HomeServices of America (Part of NYSE:BRK)
- HomeSmart
- Howard Hanna
- Keller Williams
- Opendoor
- Purplebricks (LN: PURP)
- Realogy (NYSE: RLGY)
- Redfin (NASDAQ: RDFN)
- Re/Max (NASDAQ: RMAX)
- Realty One Group

Finally, the T3 Sixty team then mapped these firms along a six-point spectrum between the two opposing aspects of each core brokerage business model element.

Location on the scale of each element carries no value judgment. Placing these representative firms along a spectrum of residential real estate brokerage's key business model elements is meant to illustrate the similarities, differences and components of each model.

The Traditional Brokerage Model

Prevalent in every ZIP code in the country, the traditional brokerage business model has been dominant since the 1950s and 60s. While many other models are listed and discussed in this chapter, this model represents more brokers in pure number (brokerages as well as agent count) than any other. Core to the traditional model are independent real estate agents working on a commission split with their broker out of neighborhood bricks-and-mortar offices. Traditional firms, of course, have many other core features, but these the two are the most notable when comparing them to newer models.

Real Estate Brokerage Business Model Landscape

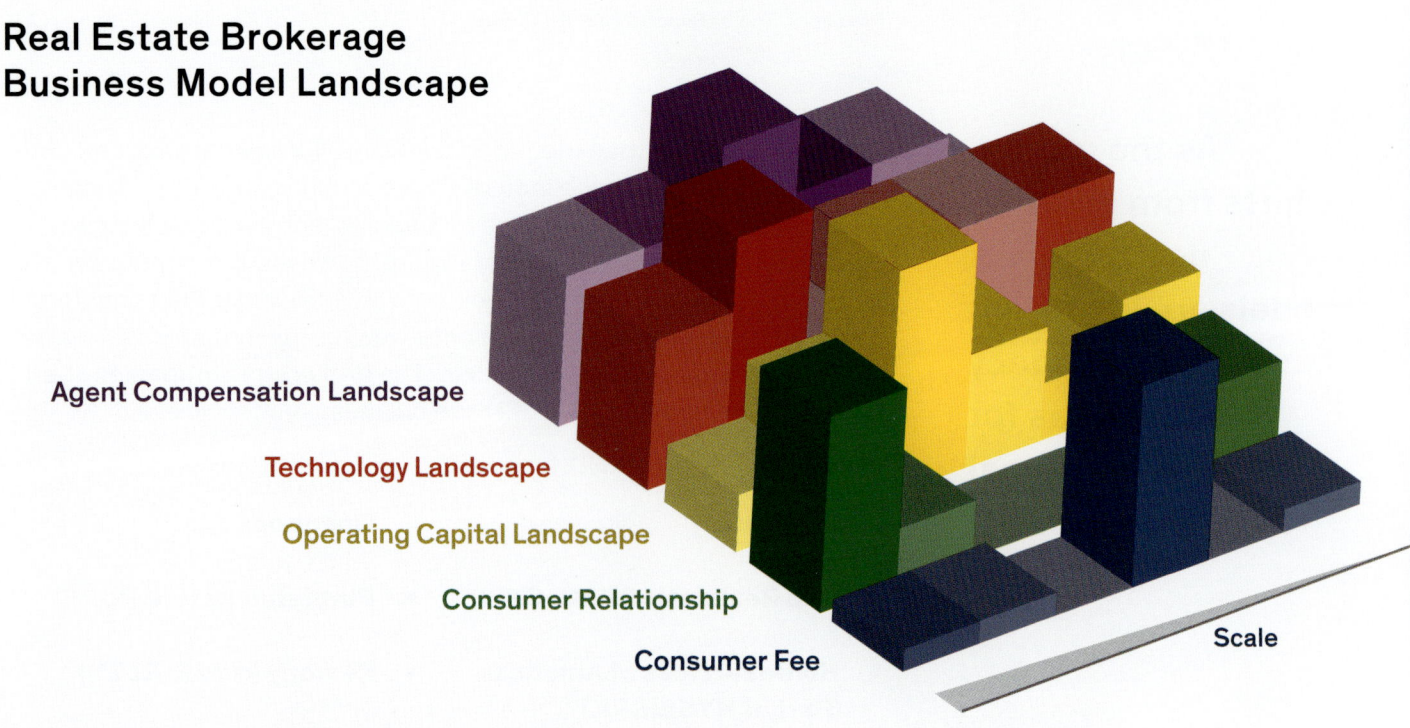

Agent Compensation Landscape
Technology Landscape
Operating Capital Landscape
Consumer Relationship
Consumer Fee
Scale

The Real Estate Brokerage Business Model Landscape shows how the industry's predominant business models compare across five core business model elements.

Agent Compensation Landscape
Agent compensation has become a dominant and important business model differentiator, and in large part, defines a brokerage's business model. The scale ranges from models with brokers taking on higher risk related to compensation to those where agents take on more risk.

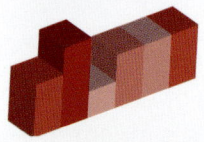

Technology Landscape
Technology has become a huge differentiating factor, and brokerages vary widely in how they incorporate and implement it. The scale ranges from models with proprietary, self-built technology to those who leverage outside tech systems.

Operating Capital Landscape
The influx of massive amounts of funding, especially from external sources, is transforming the residential real estate brokerage industry. The operating capital scale ranges from models with larger amounts of operating capital to those that have less.

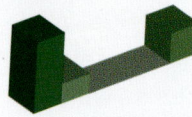

Consumer Relationship
Traditional brokerages do not typically work with consumers directly while some newer brokerages cultivate strong, direct relationships with consumers. The scale ranges from the traditional relationship (average) to a new direct relationship (high).

Consumer Fee
The consumer fee scale plots models across their various consumer fee types. The scale ranges from models with lower consumer fees to those with higher consumer fees.

Source: T3 Sixty

Note:
Locations on the scale of each element carries no value judgement. Neither the left or right side is better than the other. Placement is relative to each other in order to illustrate strengths, and compare similarities.

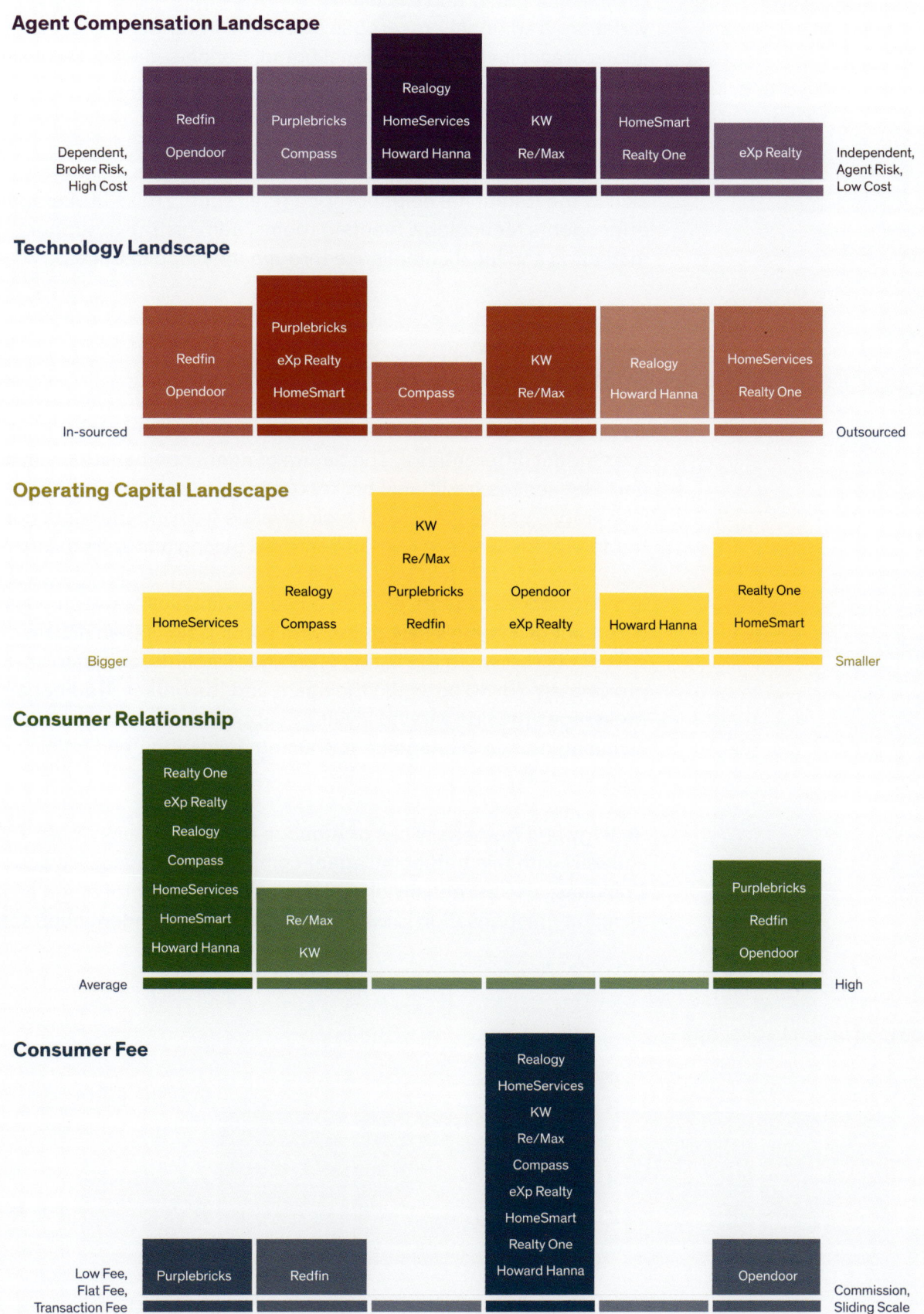

Source: T3 Sixty

Given its longevity and popularity, the traditional model has a lot of variation. Traditional brokerages also come in various sizes and affiliations: franchised with a national brand, franchised with a regional or local brand, large independent all the way down to small one-or-two-person shops.

Most often featuring bricks-and-mortar local offices, the model is akin to the traditional neighborhood retail shop. These brokerages offer agents technology, meeting rooms, administrative support, marketing and legal compliance through these local offices.

Agent Compensation

Agent compensation has become a dominant and important business model differentiator. The nature of agent compensation, in large part, defines the traditional brokerage business model. Traditional brokerages derive the bulk of their revenue from independent contractor agents who provide conventional buying and selling services.

In most markets, agents provide these services for between 5 and 6 percent of a home's sale price, with commissions then usually split 50-50 between the listing and buyer's agents, and then approximately 70-30 between the agent and the broker. Traditional brokerages provide varying levels of support to real estate agents – including offices, management, training technology, and admin and legal support.

Realogy and HomeServices of America brokerages align most squarely with this traditional agent compensation model. Newcomer Compass, also essentially operates as a traditional brokerage as far as agent compensation is concerned; it has independent contractor

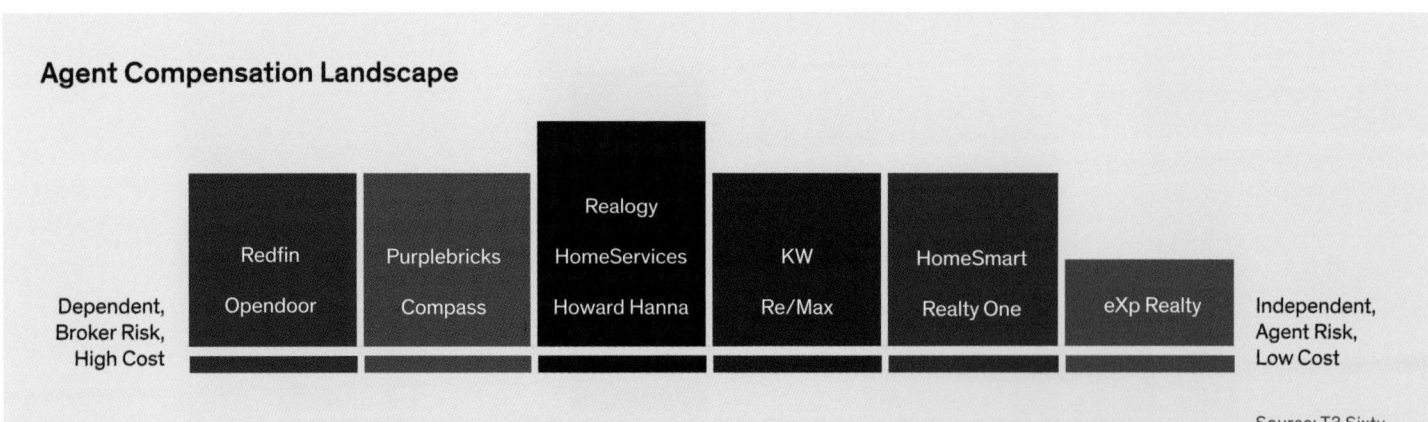

Source: T3 Sixty

agents on a traditional split — its splits, however, have crept higher toward the agent as it looks to attract top talent in its sustained growth spurt.

The other firms have variations of this model. Agents with Re/Max — the dominant, and one of the pioneers of the 100 percent model — pay a monthly management fee in exchange for keeping all (or the bulk) of their commissions. High agent commission splits are a hallmark of the Re/Max business model.

Keller Williams and eXp Realty, while using traditional splits, have annual commission caps, beyond which agents no longer share commission with their brokerage. Once agents' compensation contributions to the brokerage surpass a predetermined amount in a given year, they keep 100 percent of their commissions. In some cases, a portion of the fees paid to the broker are channeled back to the agents through profit- or revenue-sharing arrangements.

> "Companies with this model tend to leverage technology more than traditional brokerages."

A modern variant of the Re/Max business model entered the industry in the early 2000s. In this business model, agents keep all of their commission; instead of sharing with their broker, they pay a monthly fee (often referred to as a membership fee) and, often, also a transaction fee. This model is often called the agent flat fee or agent fixed fee model; the Re/Max model is often referred to as the 100 percent business model. Popularized by companies such as Realty One Group and HomeSmart, this model has lower margins than traditional firms and requires high growth and lots of agents to thrive.

Companies with this model tend to leverage technology more than traditional brokerages. Agent support, however, is typically more a one-size-fits-all, templated and automated structure. This is both a strong plus for an industry in dire need of more uniformity and a big challenge because of its depersonalized flavor. The industry only has room for a handful of these firms so current forerunners likely have this segment of the market cornered. For more on this model, see Trend No. 3 in the *2017 Swanepoel Trends Report*, "Agent Flat-Fee Brokerages on the Rise."

Newcomer, Purplebricks, has a mix of independent contractor agents and in-house employee agents. The number of independent contractor agents, who tend to handle consumers in the field, vastly outnumber in-house employee agents. Because Purplebricks has a focus on generating leads for agents, it shares commissions with agents at a 60-40 split, with the larger portion going to the real estate agent.

To the far left of the agent compensation spectrum lie brokerages who largely use salaried agents. These brokerages receive and keep

eXp Realty in Review

A pioneer of the virtual brokerage model, eXp Realty has been on a growth tear in recent years. From approximately 2,500 agents in early 2017 it grew agent count fivefold to over 13,000 in September 2018. The public firm also moved from a smaller stock market to the NASDAQ in 2018, achieving an over $1 billion valuation in the process.

The national firm has no brick-and-mortar offices and instead has built an immersive 3D virtual environment where brokerage leaders, agents and staff meet and collaborate. The virtual world is not the key attraction of the model for agents, however. Instead, they are attracted by the firm's generous 80-20 commission split and its annual commission cap of $16,000. The company also offers revenue share to agents who recruit agents to the firm. Agents can also earn company stock.

Besides lowering its overhead, the virtual model allows eXp Realty to expand at low cost. It can enter markets without a big capital investment or long lead time. To support its virtual business, the firm uses a variety of tools including a team collaboration tool called Workplace by Facebook, digital transaction management tool SkySlope and lead generation and CRM platform Inside Real Estate.

Overview
Founded by Glenn Sanford in 2009, eXp Realty has shot up in recent years. It began trading on Nasdaq in 2018, with a valuation of over $1 billion. It has grown agent count to over 13,000 in 2018, representing a more than 500 percent jump from early 2017.

Geographic Presence
49 states, three Canadian provinces.

Size
Over 13,000 agents, 60,000 transactions totalling more than with $15 billion in sales volume.

all the commissions in a transaction; they primarily compensate agents with a fixed compensation structure, often with incentives for certain achievements, such as how consumers rate them and the price range of the homes they help sell. Redfin is the most prominent of the firms in this group.

The new, Direct Buyer model (also known as iBuyers), as exemplified by Opendoor, also uses this agent-compensation method. A growing cadre of large traditional brokerage companies such as Realogy and Keller Williams Realty, have recently announced adding Direct Buyer models to their offering. The traditional firms will likely use their own agents to serve their Direct Buyer clients, possibly on a modified traditional split, where they keep more of the commission for owning the client relationship and managing the process. The same way traditional brokerages changed the 50-50 compensation structure of the 1960s to a sliding scale in the 1970s and 80s, to combat their losses against the growth of Re/Max. They are again adapting to complete against the Direct Buyer phenomenon.

Technology

Technology has become a huge differentiating factor in brokerage business models, and brokerages vary widely in how they incorporate and implement it. Brokerage companies who have been around for longer periods, such as HomeServices of America, Realogy, Keller Williams Realty and Re/Max, have always used some degree of technology, and have updated their technology periodically to accommodate shifting trends. For large companies adopting new technology can be, of course, a slower and more complicated process.

> "Most often, it is not what a business does but how."

Newer brokerages, especially those pioneering innovative, newer models such as Redfin, Opendoor and Purplebricks have built their businesses significantly on or around modern technology. Their models depend on technology and are built to leverage it in as many ways as they possibly can. During the first years of their launch, this gave them a huge advantage, but slowly traditional brokerages are catching up. So, it is no longer about the tech, but how a well-conceived technology strategy is implemented. Effective technology roll-outs will next determine the brokerage winners of tomorrow.

Some legacy companies are making big bold tech moves. Keller Williams Realty now describes itself as a technology company and is focusing a lot of its energy, and cash, on building out its tech wing KW Labs. It released its voice-activated virtual assistant Kelle in 2018 and is working on enhancing it with artificial intelligence.

COMPASS

Compass in Review

Compass has a stated goal to secure 20 percent market share in the country's top twenty markets by 2020. This is an ambitious goal that will be difficult to achieve as existing market share players push back. However, its cash sings and could lead to a few more large acquisitions.

Compass has told a tech-backed story since its launch, but the tech platform it says it is building in-house has yet to produce meaningful results, by many reports. The company has 500 non-agents (engineers, designers, marketers) working to improve technology and marketing for the company and its agents.

Currently, its technology includes the following products for agents: Insights (listing performance reports), Collections (co-shopping with agents and consumers), and a Marketing Center. It also has two consumer iOS mobile apps. In November 2017, the company announced a plan to develop a custom CRM platform, something it has talked about since launch.

The firm is racing to secure market share by acquiring brokerages, teams and top-producing agents. It often attracts the latter two with huge signing bonuses, which in some cases stretch into the six figures. It is also tempts top-producing agents with friendly splits and stock options.

Overview
Launched in 2012, closed $25 million in venture funding in 2013, expanded to Washington D.C., and raised $42 million in 2014, grew agent count above 2,000 and raises a game-changing $550 million for a $2.2 billion valuation in 2017. Acquired Pacific Union International and raises $400 million in 2018.

Geographic Presence
17 markets and counting. Markets include San Francisco, Los Angeles, Boston, New York City, Washing D.C., Miami and Chicago.

Size
Approximately 4,000 agents and over $28 billion in annual sales (includes sales volume of Pacific Union).

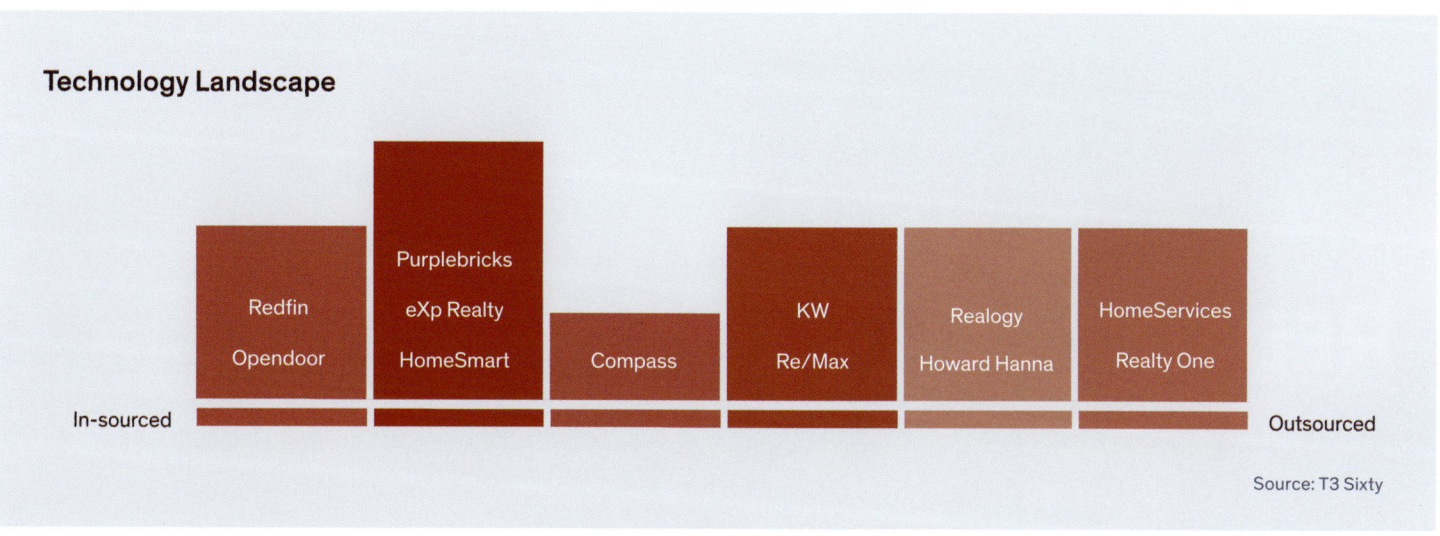

Realogy bought tech brokerage ZipRealty in 2014 for $166 million and transformed it into its tech hub ZapLabs. In 2018, Re/Max acquired real estate marketing technology firm, booj, to up its tech offering to franchisees and agents and Howard Hanna is an investor in brokerage tech platform Moxi Works.

For insight into how to build and institute a smart brokerage technology strategy, see Trend No. 3, "The Technology Conundrum."

Brokerage Operating Capital

The influx of massive amounts of funding, especially from external sources, is transforming the residential real estate brokerage industry in many different ways. For example, thanks to over $1.2 billion in funding, six-year-old Compass has bought its way to the top of the brokerage charts (see mega1000.com). With its 2018 acquisition of Pacific Union International, it is now the nation's third-largest brokerage, by 2017 annual sales volume!

Most, if not all, large firms have access to funds but the amounts at their disposal differ greatly; here is where the difference is most visible.

As a subsidiary of public holding company giant Berkshire Hathaway — whose market cap exceeds $530 billion — HomeServices of America has access to the greatest amount of capital. Its 2017 blockbuster acquisition of Long &Foster Real Estate, then the third largest firm in the country by annual sales volume, illustrates this. The company stands in a class of its own.

Realogy and Compass make up the next tier. Publicly held Realogy

REDFIN

Redfin in Review

Redfin leads with its powerful consumer technology, marked by its sleek and fast national website, which, with a monthly average of 28.7 million unique visitors in the second quarter 2018, is by far the nation's most popular brokerage website. The sleek technology, which includes a powerful, popular mobile app, serves as a customer acquisition and retention tool.

Overview
Founded in 2004, launched in 2006, expanded nationally in 2015, went public in July 2017. Raised $239 million in a debt and stock offering in 2018. It runs a Direct Buyer model under the RedfinNow brand.

Geographic Presence
All 50 states, over 80 markets.

Size
Over $22 billion in annual sales in 2017 and over 1,400 lead agents as of June 2018.

Discounts are a big part of its consumer value proposition and branding. It offers a one percent listing fee in twenty-six markets and a 1.5 listing fee in its over fifty others. The 1 percent listing fee covers 80 percent of its homesellers. It also offers buyers rebates, which averaged $2,700 in 2017.

In July 2018, it raised $239 million through a mixed debt and stock offering. The firm did not outline how it would use the funds, but hinted at possible acquisitions. Redfin uses a combination of lead agents and support agents. Lead agents work primarily with clients; desk-bound support agents fill in gaps and answer questions. Both are full-time employees. Before going public in July 2017, it raised over $200 million in equity funding that it used to build a sleek brokerage technology stack that it continues to build out. The brokerage has been a full-fledged tech company since launch.

Some of its key technology includes the ability to make draft offers from their smartphone, with Redfin's agent-focused mobile app, its automated valuation model Redfin Estimate and Redfin Hot Homes, which uses artificial intelligence to alert buyers to homes, that big data suggests, will likely sell soon. Some of Redfin's newer services include an in-house mortgage operation that adds to its other owned ancillary Title and Escrow service, Title Forward. It also has a Direct Buyer division, RedfinNow, which it implemented formally in 2018 after running it as an experiment. It upped its RedfinNow budget from $25 million to $35 million in July 2018. While Redfin does not have significant share in any one market, it was the nation's fourth largest brokerage in 2018.

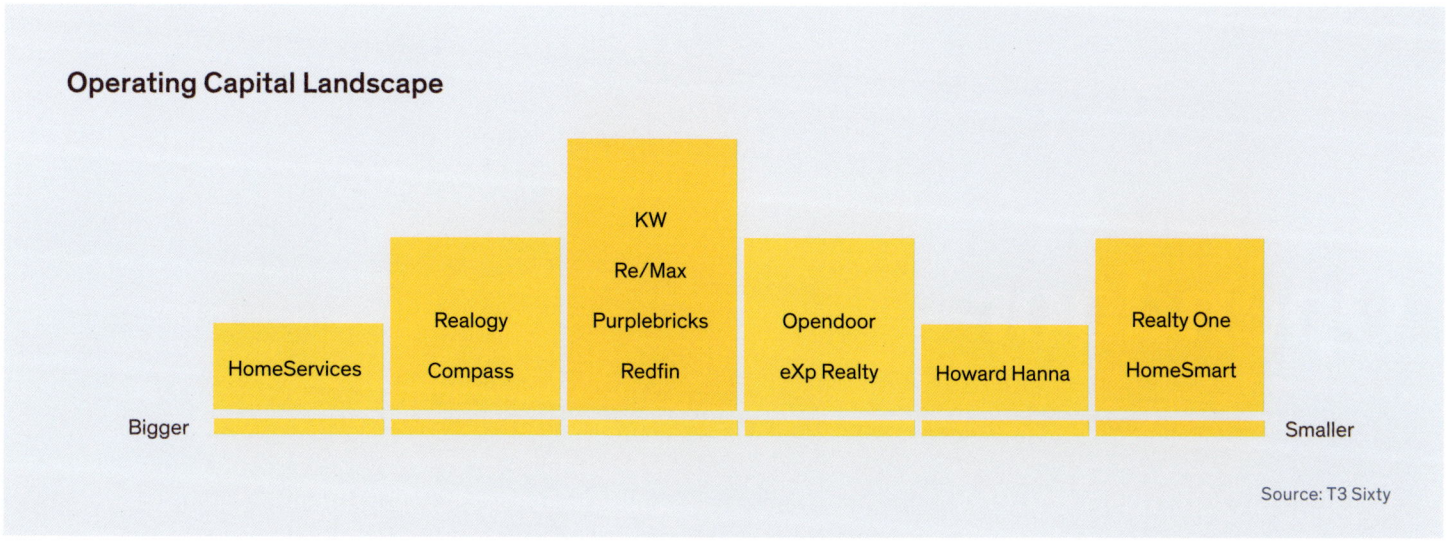

not only has access to funding, the company also annually rakes in approximately $400 million in profit on $6 billion in revenue. Newcomer and venture capital darling Compass, and its seemingly bottomless investor appeal, has demonstrated access to disproportionately large amounts of funding.

All but one of the companies in the next tier are public companies — see Redfin, Re/Max and Purplebricks — and can raise large amounts of cash from selling company shares to the public market. The outlier on this list is Keller Williams (KW), who is now the largest privately owned residential real estate brokerage company/brand. Although it has not taken on outside funding, the group has significant funds at its disposal as the US leader in annual sales volume. It has also shown a commitment to use it.

For example, KW pledged $1 billion to developing technology, some of it deployed to develop its virtual assistant Kelle and to make acquisitions such as real estate agent app developer Smarter Agent (smarteragent.com), in September 2018, and team lead generation platform Team Leads Inc., in August 2018.

With a September 2018 raise of $400 million from Softbank, Opendoor is proving it, too, has access to vast amounts of capital. It has raised a total of $1.045 billion in equity financing through September 2018; in addition, it has secured $2 billion in debt financing, which allows the firm to hold that value of housing at any one time, a key asset for its Direct Buyer business model. Newcomer eXp Realty has risen rapidly from a penny stock to a billion dollar market capitalization.

Howard Hanna, Realty One Group and HomeSmart have smaller war chests than those mentioned above, but they have enough to make

> "Hubris so often plays a big role in leaderboard shake-ups, but it is not the only driver. Each innovation cycle sees the game shift — often status quo operations do not fit the new eras."

Opendoor

Opendoor in Review

Opendoor put the Direct Buyer brokerage business model on the map when it launched in Phoenix in 2015 and began raising increasing amounts of cash. In 2018 alone, it raised $725 million.

Firms with this model, which now include Redfin, Realogy and Keller Williams Realty, aim to take the uncertainty and hassle out of homeselling by presenting sellers purchase offers, in many cases within 24 hours, and allow them to specify closing dates in as soon as three days of an accepted offer.

Direct Buyers purchase homes themselves, then prep them for sale and become sellers themselves. They streamline the buying process by offering buyers on-demand access to their homes and easy offer options. Some question whether the model will work in markets with wide variations in inventory, at higher prices or when the market turns.

By the end of 2018, Opendoor will be in eighteen US markets with plans to be in fifty markets by 2020.

Overview
Founded in mid-2014, launched in June 2015 in Phoenix, and in 2018 raised $725 million, acquired discount brokerage Open Listings and is vigorously expanding. It expects to be in 18 markets by the end of 2018. In August 2018, the firm bought over 1,000 homes, more than twice the amount it did a year previous.

Geographic Presence
It is in 16 markets including Phoenix, Atlanta, Denver, Las Vegas and Minneapolis. It plans to be live in 18 markets by the end of 2018.

Size
Buying homes at a rate of over 1,000 homes per month. It expects to nearly double its employee count in 2018 to end the year with over 1,000 employees.

interesting and meaningful moves. Howard Hanna's September 2018 acquisition of large mid-Atlantic brokerage Allen Tate Companies, the nation's 27th largest brokerage, is one such example.

For more on the funding of rapidly changing residential real estate, see Trend No. 1 in the *2018 Swanepoel Trends Report*, "Follow The Money."

Consumer Relationship

Traditional brokerages do not typically work with consumers directly; instead, they primarily interact with consumers through their agents. This is one way some of the new business models are changing the industry: by cultivating strong, direct relationships with consumers.

This brokerage model element displays the most stark difference among current brokerages. At least currently, brokerages either aim to form direct relationships with consumers or primarily serve consumers through their agents. There is not much in-between. This, of course, could change as firms test out new ways to adapt and build hybrid models.

This move to build closer relationships with consumers began with the rise of the web, when online real estate took off and real estate began playing a more central cultural role marked by popular reality TV shows and the automated valuation model popularized by Zillow's Zestimate.

As portals took off, generating leads online became a new and viable way to establish and grow a real estate business. The rise of both digital marketing and online real estate gave brokerages powerful new

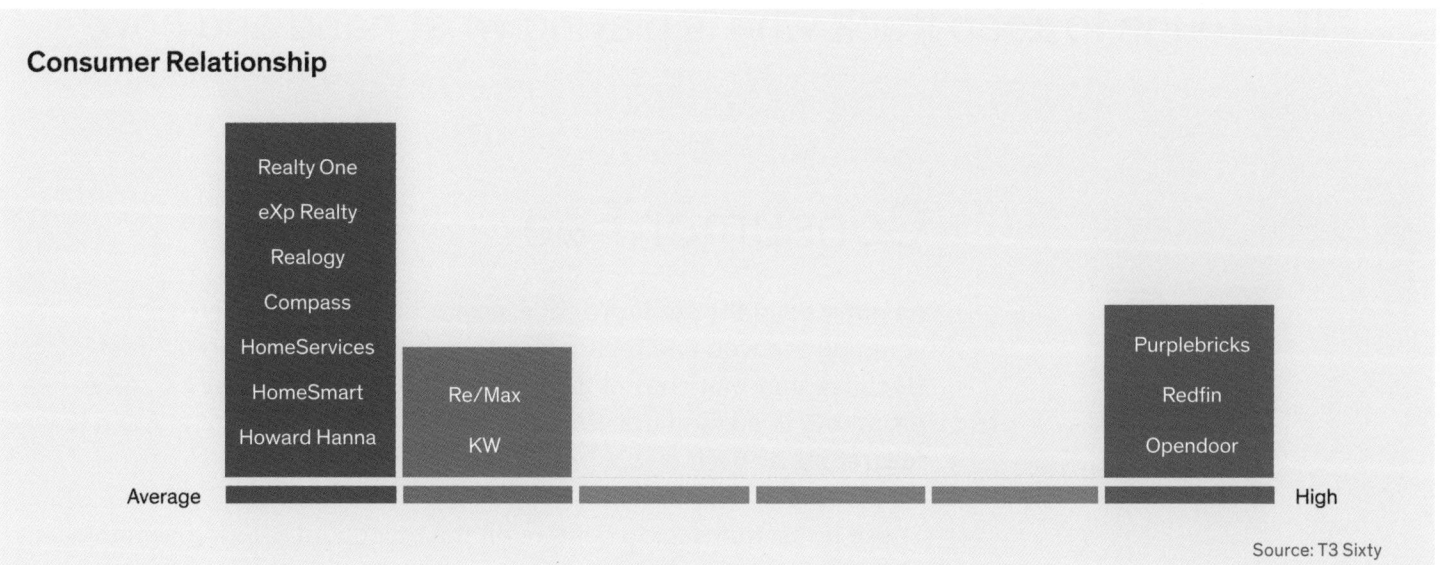

ways to form direct relationships with consumers. Newer brokerages such as Redfin, Opendoor and Purplebricks have squarely focused on forming closer relationships with consumers, serving as the primary point of contact from lead to contract to close and beyond. They do this with a mix of employee agents, streamlined technology that gives consumers access to parts of the search and transaction process and well-honed procedures.

Because they have agent employees, these firms tend to own the connections with consumers. Along with new ways of transacting as epitomized by the Direct Buyer model, some of these firms offer consumer discounts, which tend to be higher on the list side. Because many of these firms have in-house agents, they can dictate operations and agent service to a much larger degree than brokerages who use independent contractor agents. This leads to efficiency and tight operations with predictable levels of consumer service. But it can also dampen agents' enthusiasm for customer service, as this short-circuits the drive, pride and motivation that comes with entrepreneurship.

Brokerages with a direct-to-consumer model have modern technology as a core feature. Typically, technology is built in-house and centers on optimizing customer acquisition, operations and helping consumers participate in the homebuying and homeselling process, from making offers to touring homes. Agents at brokerages with more traditional models typically set their own fees, which consumers can negotiate. These fees tend to hover between 5 to 6 percent of the purchase price. Buyer and seller agents often split that commission 50-50. This is the predominant brokerage consumer fee model.

"It is tough to keep track who is playing what hand and how."

Consumer Fee

As outlined in the section above, newer brokerage models are leveraging the web and technology to own the consumer relationship. Because they can control the consumer experience, they can offer discounts to consumers. Primarily, these take the form of either a flat fee, rebate or both.

These firms' messaging centers on their discount offering, whether

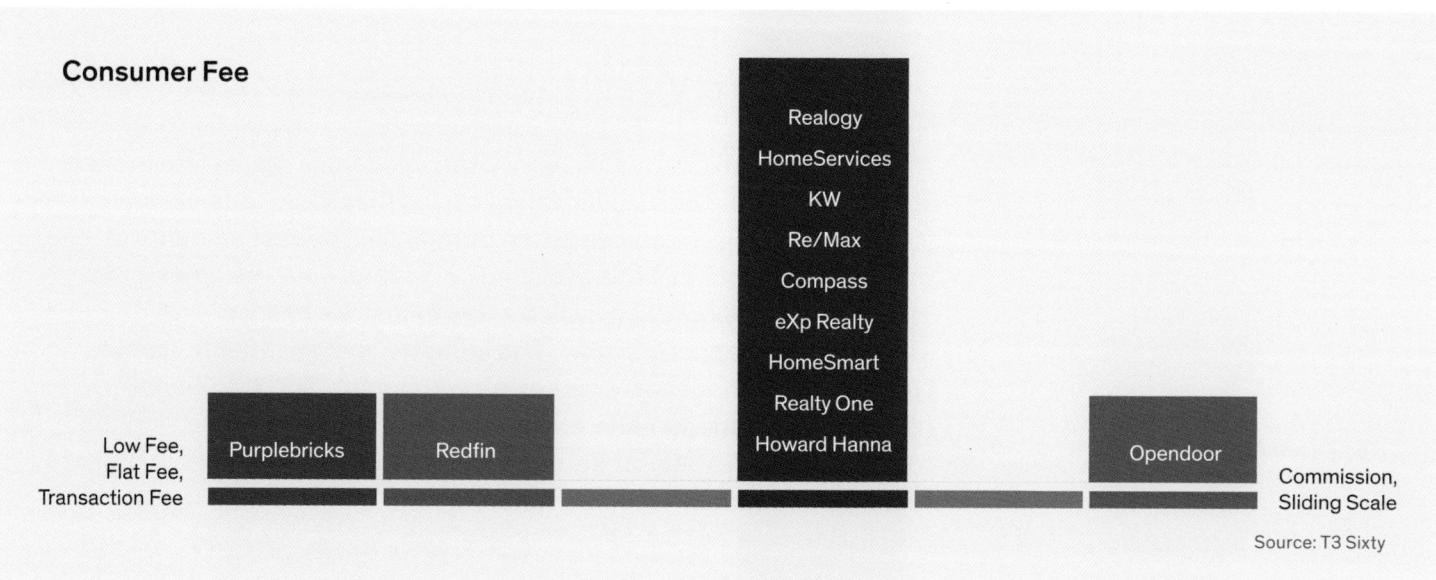

Source: T3 Sixty

it be a flat listing fee or buyer rebate. Redfin, for example, has been prominently marketing its 1 percent listing fee in the markets where it offers it. Purplebricks lists sellers' homes for a flat fee of $3,200 and provides qualifying buyers a rebate of $1,000, and promotes the discount prominently on its website: "List for a low fixed fee."

Even with lower fees, discount brokerages market full real estate service to consumers. Given that they showcase relatively complete digital marketing for listings and task-based buyer services, they are not inaccurate. However, higher levels of service typically involve the deep knowledge of experienced real estate agents who have the time to dive into clients' specific needs. This is not always clear to consumers; some, of course, do not need or want that deeper level of service.

For a detailed analysis on the discount brokerage model, see Trend No. 3 in the *2018 Swanepoel Trends Report*, "Rise of the Modern Discount Brokerage."

The new Direct Buyer models used by Opendoor, and others including Redfin and, recently, Realogy and Keller Williams Realty, impacts the consumer-pricing percentage. Instead of charging traditional commissions between 5 to 6 percent, they charge sellers a listing fee that ranges from approximately 6 percent to up to 10 percent. The fees these firms charge vary as do the specific way they operate it; as it is still very new, they are still experimenting with the business model and the amount consumers are willing pay.

At the lower range, these fees come close to matching the traditional commission fee. But these firms often offer sellers prices below what they could get if the property sold through the open market.

Takeaway

As T3 Sixty chronicles in this report, the residential real estate brokerage industry proceeds in innovation cycles that span 13 to 18 years (see Trend No. 10 "Gradually, Then Suddenly). The vast amounts of funding and velocity of this cycle indicates that it may be among the most impactful innovation cycles in the industry's history.
The impact is happening now. The industry is at an inflection point. New business models are jockeying with legacy and traditional brokerages for market share. This competition is reengineering the residential real estate brokerage industry and redefining how brokers and agents serve buyers and sellers.

"Innovation is coming faster and furious. Get ready. It is game on!"

It is too soon to tell what models will win. Therefore, brokers and agents must remain on their toes, to keep their ears to the ground and focused on remaining knowledgeable and implementing smart strategies.

The first step involves orientation, the next, bold action. This chapter should help brokers with the former. A mix of smarts and gumption will help them with the next step. Innovation is coming faster and furious. Get ready. It is game on!

Lead Contributors:

Stefan Swanepoel
Stefan, Chairman and CEO of T3 Sixty, is widely recognized as the leading visionary on real estate trends. With over 35 years of experience in the real estate industry, he served as CEO of nine companies and two nonprofit organizations. He has authored or co-authored over forty books including the Swanepoel Trends Report, Swanepoel Power 200 and Swanepoel Mega 1000. Stefan can be reached at stefan@t360.com.

Paul Hagey
Paul is Executive Editor of the Swanepoel Trends Report, founding Publisher of Boulder, Colorado, magazine BLDRfly and runs the content agency HageyMedia. He began covering the real estate in-dustry as fulltime reporter with Inman News, where he became an award-winning journalist. Paul is a graduate of the University of Missouri Graduate School of Journalism. Paul can be reached at paul@t360.com.

T3 Summit

The leading invite-only leadership think-tank event for CEOs and C-level executives in real estate.

2019 T3 Summit • May 6-8, 2019 • San Diego, CA

t3summit.com
t360.com

Stefan Swanepoel, CEO
stefan@t360.com
(949) 202-5758

Jack Miller, President
jack@t360.com
(512) 772-4341

Tinus Swanepoel, COO
tinus@t360.com
(949) 397-2107

(949) 627-8877
t360.com

About T3 Sixty

Since 1997, we have identified and analyzed hundreds of trends, business models and shifts that have impacted the residential real estate industry. Many were accurately detailed years before they became part of the mainstream.

Our suite of regular reports and studies include:

- Swanepoel Trends Report (annually since 2006)
- Swanepoel Power 200 (annually since 2014)
- Swanepoel Mega 1000 (annually since 2018)

We have also published dozens of white papers and case studies since 1999, including major national studies such as:

- The Definitive Analysis of Negative Game Changes Emerging in Real Estate (DANGER Report)
- The Canadian DANGER Report
- The Commercial Real Estate Analysis of the Latest Emerging Risks and Trends (CRE ALERT)
- The MLS 2020 Agenda

T3 Sixty does not create the news. We do not report the news. We analyze the news, understand why it happens and what impact it may have. We help reduce the noise in the real estate industry, so you can make better decisions.

Understanding innovation, change and new business models in real estate, especially before the rest of your competition, enables you to create strategies that give you an advantage. Countless companies have ignored change and suffered the consequences. Don't be one of them.

Although no one can exactly predict the future, you can find double-digit growth if you know where to look. Constant exploration and systematic analysis provides insights that can be as valuable as market intelligence, if not more.

And that is what T3 Sixty provides business leaders: a multidisciplined and experienced consulting team focused on finding the answers and solving problems.

If you would like to explore how you can leverage T3 Sixty to your benefit, let's have a confidential conversation to explore your options.